PEBBLES

of

PRAYER

and

PONDERINGS

Blessings,
Patricia

Romans 11:36

PEBBLES

of

PRAYER

and

PONDERINGS

Patricia Van Gorder

TATE PUBLISHING
AND ENTERPRISES, LLC

Published by Tate Publishing & Enterprises, LLC
127 E. Trade Center Terrace | Mustang, Oklahoma 73064 USA
1.888.361.9473 | www.tatepublishing.com

Tate Publishing is committed to excellence in the publishing industry. The company reflects the philosophy established by the founders, based on Psalm 68:11,

"The Lord gave the word and great was the company of those who published it."

Book design copyright © 2016 by Tate Publishing, LLC. All rights reserved.
Cover design by Samson Lim
Interior design by Manolito Bastasa

Published in the United States of America

ISBN: 978-1-68237-156-5
Religion / Christian Life / Devotional
15.10.27

To my devoted husband, Larry.
Softly, gently, we slipped into each other's
lives, and friendship blossomed into love.
We are best friends.
Our love is a precious gift, and God is the
fulfillment of our dedication to each other.
He is our foundation and our anchor. He *is* love.

INTRODUCTION

I PREFER A pristine, hard-packed sand beach for my walk. But some days, rocks are deposited along the shore. It's not easy walking over a rock pile.

Some of these rocks are fragments cut from shore lined jagged cliffs and craggy boulders that have been pounded by relentless thunderous tides. Little by little the pebbles have been chiseled, sculptured, rolled, and tumbled until they are smooth.

They've not been shaped in a day but are the ocean's response to a process that has taken countless years.

I pick one up, close my eyes, and hear only the crashing waves headed toward me. As I finger the solid smooth surface, I feel God's distinctive presence with me on my bit of beach.

I think about myself as a fragment of what God would have me be. Like the pebble, I am being sculptured, rolled, and tumbled.

Little did I dream that on a July afternoon twenty-six years ago, God would bring me to this edge of the Pacific Ocean. With generous pleasure, He fulfilled my dream of living at the water.

The first time I stepped onto the Solana Beach shore, I could not have imagined how important this strand of beach would become. I could not envision the hundreds of hours He would accompany me down the beach and the lessons He would teach me along the way. Even after all these years, the exciting reality of His immeasurable power brought to life through the sea, sand, and sun stirs within me.

One day He will take me home, and I will leave this water's edge. The vibrant life of the sea and all of its gifts will be left for others to discover. I pray that here too they will garner pebbles of prayer and ponderings.

January 1

> But, beloved, do not forget this one thing, that
> with the Lord one day *is* as a thousand years, and a
> thousand years as one day.
>
> —2 Peter 3:8, NKJV

The month of January is named after the mythological Roman god Janus. He was usually portrayed with two faces looking in opposite directions: one looking behind and the other looking forward. The name of Janus was derived from the Latin word *janua*, which means "a door."

New Year's Day brings memories of the past year and hopes for the future. Sad events intermingle with recollections of happy moments. Something inside is ready to move on to promises of better times, yet we linger in the bittersweet of yesterday.

We know that Jesus doesn't change. He is the same yesterday, today, and forever. No matter what befalls us in this earthly life, He is constant! His sovereignty is, was, and always will be. He is the Door to this New Year.

> Glory to God in highest heaven,
> Who unto man His Son hath given;

While angels sing with tender mirth,
A glad new year to all the earth.

—Martin Luther

January 2

To everything there is a season.

—Ecclesiastes 3:1, NASB

Lord God, reveal Your plans for me this year. Give me the wisdom to accomplish all things that will please You and bring You glory.

May I live moment by moment aware of Your presence dwelling in me.

Inspire me, most Holy God.

The world tries to rob me of joy and peace. I want to focus on You, not on the violence and evil.

I am inadequate to handle anything on my own. I need You! Some of what happens this year—the choices and decisions I make—will be of my own making. I can't control all circumstances, but I can control how I will face them. With You!

I am grateful for this season of my life. I embrace the changes and growth it will bring. All seasons are from You, and my hope and expectations lie in You!

January 3

> With my whole being, body and soul, I will shout
> joyfully to the living God.
>
> —Psalm 84:2, NLT

What joy for me to live in Your house, always singing Your praises (Ps. 84:4, NLT).

My strength comes from You.

You are my sun and shield, and You supply me with Your grace and glory.

You withhold no good thing from me, my King and my God.

I am filled with joy, for I trust in You.

I sing praise for Your glory!

By Your mighty power at work within me,

You are able to accomplish infinitely more than I can ask or think (Eph. 3:20, NLT).

You supply all I need.

I know You can do anything.

I see how much You love me, for You call me Your child.

January 4

> O Lord, *You are* the portion of my
> inheritance and my cup.
>
> —Psalm 16:5, NKJV

I will bless You for You guide me; even at night my heart instructs me. I know You are always with me.

I will not be shaken, for You are right beside me. No wonder my heart is glad and I rejoice. My body rests in safety. You will show me the way of life granting me the joy of Your presence and the pleasure of living with You forever (Ps. 16:7–9, 11).

I sing to You my Lord and my God; I will shout joyfully, for You are the Rock of my salvation. I come to You in thanksgiving.

I sing Your praises, for You are a great King, and You hold the depth of the earth and the mightiest mountains in Your hand. The sea belongs to You, for You made it.

I will kneel and bow down, worshiping You my Lord, my Maker, for You are God. You watch over me and care for me (Ps. 95:1–5, NLT).

I will listen to Your voice today!

January 5

> Be strong and of good courage, and do *it;* do not
> fear nor be dismayed, for the Lord God—my
> God—*will be* with you.
>
> —1 Chronicles 28:20, NKJV

The year begins, and all its pages are as blank as the silent years of the life of Jesus Christ.

Let us begin it with high resolution, then let us take all its limitations, all its hindrances, its disappointments, its narrow and commonplace conditions, and meet them as the Master did in Nazareth: with patience, with obedience, putting ourselves in cheerful subjection, serving our apprenticeship.

Who knows what opportunity may come to us this year? Let us live in a great spirit, and then we shall be ready for a great occasion.[1]

> Help us, O Lord! Behold we enter
> Upon another year today;
> In Thee our hopes and thoughts, now center,
> Renew our courage for the way;
> New life, new strength, new happiness,
> We ask of Thee, Oh hear, and bless! (Johann Rist)

January 6

Watch, stand fast in the faith, be brave; be strong.

—1 Corinthians 16:13, NKJV

When we surrender all that is past to His care, He will give us renewed energy, joy, courage, and peace for what lies ahead.

If we have felt the sting of sorrow, loss, struggles with addiction, illness, physical pain, mental anguish, loneliness, or grief, we might recall how God has used the difficulty to seek Him ever more fervently. We know we cannot rely on ourselves to conquer the physical and natural orders of our existence.

Our Creator can enable us to overcome any obstacle that hinders our relationship with Him. "Don't be afraid," He said. "Take courage! I am here!" (Mark 6:50, NLT)

> Here's a clean year, a white year.
> Reach your hand and take it.
> You are the builder and no one else can make it.
> See what it is that waits here, whole and new;
> It's not a year only, but a world for you. (Mary Carolyn Davies)

January 7

> No one tears a piece of cloth from a new garment
> and uses it to patch an old garment. For then the
> new garment would be ruined, and the new patch
> wouldn't even match the old garment.
>
> —Luke 5:36, NLT

Wineskins were goatskins sewed together to make watertight wine bags. Since new wine expands as it ferments, the old wineskin would rupture if new wine was added.

Jesus had come with a new message and it didn't fit into the rigid religious system of rules and traditions that the Jews followed. He didn't intend to add the new to the old.

He taught forgiveness and reconciliation with God. "What is the greatest commandment of the law?" a lawyer asked, trying to trap Him. There were over six hundred laws on the books, and the Pharisees couldn't decide which was the most important. Jesus said to him, "'You shall love the LORD your God with all your heart, with all your soul, and with all your mind.' This is *the* first and great commandment. And *the* second *is* like it: 'You shall love your neighbor as yourself'" (Matt. 22:36–39, NLT).

How many of us are steeped in rigid ritual? Do we attend the service that has "our kind of music?" Do we critique the sermon or attentively listen to the message? Is someone sitting in our pew?

Child, open your heart so wide that it will burst with joy and excitement as I fill you with My love. Your cup will overflow with love, filling the saucer!

Be pliable. My message is as vital today as it was when I delivered it on earth. Don't harden your heart or close your ears like those who rejected Me. Love Me heart, soul, and mind.

January 8

"Always remember these three little words," I told my husband as friendship blossomed into relationship. "Subject to change." Rarely a week goes by that those words don't ring true.

It is good to make plans, but they can be rearranged or cancelled without notice. The most important element of the plan is to include God's will at the center. We don't know what our life will be like by the end of our day, let alone by tomorrow.

We can write our list of things to do, map out the day or the week, schedule appointments. As we fill in our calendar, maybe we should add a note: "Your will, O Lord." Everything in life is subject to change. But we can cling to His promise. "I am the Lord and I do not change" (Mal. 3:6, NLT).

No matter what happens in our life today or any day, He is the unchangeable that we can count on.

> In the dispensation of the fullness of the
> times He might gather together in one all
> things in Christ, both which are in heaven
> and which are on earth—in Him.
>
> —Ephesians 1:10, NKJV

January 9

> Yet for us there is *but* one God, the Father, from whom are all things and we *exist* for Him; and one Lord, Jesus Christ, by whom are all things, and we *exist* through Him. (1 Cor. 8:6, NASB; emphasis mine)

> All should honor the Son just as they honor the Father. He who does not honor the Son does not honor the Father who sent Him. (John 5:23, NKJV)

> After these things I looked, and behold, a great multitude which no one could number, of all nations, tribes, peoples, and tongues, standing before the throne and before the Lamb, clothed with white robes, with palm branches in their hands, and crying

out with a loud voice, saying, "Salvation *belongs* to our God who sits on the throne, and to the Lamb!"

> Blessing and glory and wisdom
> "Amen! Blessing and glory and wisdom,
> Thanksgiving and honor and power and might,
> *Be* to our God forever and ever.
> Amen. (Rev. 7:9–10, 12, NKJV)

Those of us who honor God will be in that crowd! Amen!

January 10

I praise You, Lord.

I praise You from the heavens; praise You from the skies!

I praise You with all Your angels and all the armies of heaven

I praise You as do the sun and moon and all the twinkling stars; the highest heavens and the vapors that are above the clouds!

Let every created thing give praise to You, O Lord, for You issued Your command, and they came into being. Let them give glory to the LORD, and declare His praise in the coastlands (Isa. 42:12, NKJV).

Great *is* the LORD, and greatly to be praised; and His greatness *is* unsearchable (Ps. 145:3, NKJV).

Sing songs of praise today! The song in your heart will drown out unsettling noise.

January 11

One day Jesus told His disciples a story to show that they should always pray and never give up.

There was a judge in a certain city, who neither feared God nor cared about people.

A widow of that city came to him repeatedly, saying, "Give me justice in this dispute with my enemy." The judge ignored her for a while, but finally he said to himself, 'I don't fear God or care about people, but this woman is driving me crazy. I'm going to see that she gets justice, because she is wearing me out with her constant requests!'

Then the Lord said, "Learn a lesson from this unjust judge. Even he rendered a just decision in the end. So don't you think God will surely give justice to His chosen people who cry out to Him day and night? Will He keep putting them off? I tell you, He will grant justice to them quickly! But when the Son of Man returns, how many will He find on the earth who have faith?" (Luke 18:1–8, NLT)

Live by every word that comes
from the mouth of the Lord.

—Deuteronomy 8:3, NLT

January 12

Today, Lord, I will look straight ahead and keep my eyes on what lies before me.

I will not follow the ways of the world but keep my focus on You as You lead me in the way in which You want me to go.

I trust in You with all my heart and not my own understanding.

I will acknowledge You in everything I do and look to You for direction.

I am not impressed with my wisdom. But instead I am in awe of You. I can do nothing on my own, and if I take my eyes off You, certainly I will stumble. I look ahead with confidence in what You have in store for me.

From tedious toil, from anxious care,
Dear Lord, I turn again to Thee;
Thy presence and Thy smile to share
Makes every burden light to me. (Ray Palmer)

January 13

> We who have fled to Him for refuge
> can have great confidence as we hold
> to the hope that lies before us.
>
> —Hebrews 6:18, NLT

Refugees flee their country seeking safety from the ravages of war and evil dictators. They are victims of a situation over which they have no control. They walk great distances through rugged terrain or desolate plains with little to no food or water. Earthly possessions are left behind to those who will dispose of them as they will. They arrive across borders where tents are set up providing sparse needs for living.

For us, taking refuge may be as simple as running for shelter from an unexpected spring downpour. Or it may mean fleeing the devastating results of illness or grief. All cares and daily concerns that were priority up to now disintegrate; we desperately seek a place to flee from the heartbreak and inability to cope. We run from hopelessness.

God's Word is full of promises that He will be our Refuge, our place of safety in the time of need when we feel we have nowhere else to turn.

Child, take refuge in Me. I will spread My protection over you so that you will find peace and joy in Me. I will surround You with My shield of love. Come, rest in the shadow of My wings; I, your Lord, am your Fortress, your Refuge in the days of such distress. Run to me, and you will find great confidence of hope—hope which is a strong and trustworthy anchor for your soul.

You don't need to fear anything, particularly hopelessness. Earthquakes may come, mountains may crumble into the sea. But I, the Lord of Heaven's Armies, am here for you.

January 14

> Every man *shall give* as he is able,
> according to the blessing of the Lord
> your God which He has given you.
>
> —Deuteronomy 16:17, NKJV

The Pharisees believed wealth to be proof of their righteousness. Jesus startled them with this story of the very rich man who lived in luxury while Lazarus, a poor man covered with sores, lay at his gate longing for scraps from the table. Dogs would lick his open sores.

> So it was that the beggar died, and was carried by the angels to Abraham's bosom. The rich man also died and was buried. And being in torments in

Hades, he lifted up his eyes and saw Abraham afar off and Lazarus in his bosom.

Then he cried and said, "Father Abraham, have mercy on me, and send Lazarus that he may dip the tip of his finger in water and cool my tongue; for I am tormented in this flame." But Abraham said, "Son, remember that in your lifetime you received your good things, and likewise Lazarus evil things; but now he is comforted and you are tormented. And besides all this, between us and you there is a great gulf fixed, so that those who want to pass from here to you cannot, nor can those from there pass to us."

Then he said, "I beg you therefore, father, that you would send him to my father's house, for I have five brothers that he may testify to them, lest they also come to this place of torment." Abraham said to him, "They have Moses and the prophets; let them hear them." And he said, "No, father Abraham; but if one goes to them from the dead, they will repent." But he said to him, "If they do not hear Moses and the prophets, neither will they be persuaded though one rise from the dead." (Luke 16:22–31, NKJV)

The man didn't go to hell because he was rich but because of his lack of compassion for Lazarus, leading to indifference toward another's plight.

January 15

Often I am so busy I don't think of You as I should. The challenges and pressing responsibilities can consume me.

This morning as I grab a few moments with You, I read of Your visit with Martha when she welcomed You into her home. I can't imagine the pressure she must have felt as she scurried around preparing the dinner. It was an impromptu visit; You didn't call ahead.

I am certain she wanted to impress You.

And there was Mary, her sister, who didn't lift a hand to help. Instead, she just sat at Your feet and listened to You. Martha was overwhelmed with it all; resentment toward her sister mounted.

When she couldn't stand it any longer, she said, "Lord, doesn't it seem unfair to you that my sister just sits here while I do all the work? Tell her to come and help me."

In Your gentle and loving way You said, "My dear Martha, you are worried and upset over all these details! There is only one thing worth being concerned about. Mary has discovered it, and it will not be taken away from her."

I wonder, did she say, "Yes, but…"

This morning I begin my day sitting here listening to You. Then I will attend to details (Luke 10:39–42, NLT).

January 16

I rejoice because I put my trust in You, O God

I shout for joy, because You defend me; for I love Your name.

For You, O LORD, will bless the righteous; With favor You will surround me as *with* a shield. (Ps. 5:11–12, NKJV)

I will never lose hope, and will praise You yet more and more
You will keep me in perfect peace, because my mind *is* stayed *on You,*
I will trust in You forever,
For in You O LORD, *are* everlasting strength. (Isa. 26:3–4, NKJV)

How sweet Your words taste to me; they are sweeter than honey. (Ps. 119:103, NLT)

January 17

Ponderings on prayer:

- "Prayer is asking for rain. Faith is carrying the umbrella" (Robert C. Savage).
- "Talking to men for God is a great thing, but talking to God for men is greater still" (E. M. Bounds).
- "Intercessory prayer might be defined as loving our neighbor on our knees" (Charles H. Brent).
- "The time of labor does not with me differ from the time of prayer, and in the noise and confusion of my kitchen, while several persons are at the same time calling for different things, I possess God in as great tranquility as if I were upon my knees" (Brother Lawrence).
- "Prayer is the key of the morning and the bolt of the evening" (Matthew Henry).
- "Prayer is not asking. Prayer is putting oneself in the hands of God, at His disposition, and listening to His voice in the depth of our hearts" (Mother Teresa).

January 18

> For My name shall be great among the nations
>
> —Malachi 1:11, NKJV

Child, what small act can you perform today in My name that will give Me the honor and the glory? I don't call you to travel telling the world about My message of salvation. But each day I call you to preach right where you are. You don't need a pulpit.

Tackle mundane tasks with cheerfulness. In your workplace, hand out smiles and compliments wrapped in genuine sincerity. Give a thank you to those serving you at the checkout.

What you say and do matters. Your behavior can make a difference to those who observe you. You are My message to those within reach.

I promise I am working in you, giving you the desire and power to please Me.

> Preach always and when necessary use words.
>
> —St. Francis

January 19

Who doesn't love Peter? He was a plain fisherman—impulsive, sometimes brash. If he thought it, he usually said it.

The disciples were in their boat on the Sea of Galilee. About three o'clock in the morning, a storm came up. Jesus saw they were in trouble and came walking toward them.

> When He came into view the disciples yelled, "Look! It's a ghost." Jesus called out, "Don't be afraid. It is I."
>
> Peter shouted over the raging wind, "Lord, if it is You, command me to come to You on the water."
>
> "Come," Jesus said.
>
> He had told Peter to do the impossible, and he scrambled out of the boat and walked toward Jesus. Suddenly Peter grasped the situation and panicked. He began to sink. "Lord, save me!" Jesus took his hand and said to him, "You have little faith, Peter. Why did you doubt?" (Matt. 14:25–31, NASB)

Jesus didn't rebuke him until after He had rescued him. He then took him back to the safety of the boat. In his fear Peter had taken his eyes off Jesus and focused on what was happening around him. His first reaction was a leap of faith—that he could walk on water. And he did. But in fear his faith wavered, and he needed rescue.

We vacillate between letting God handle things and our taking charge.

In those moments of fear and indecision, we reach for Him as Peter did. Then we waver and take our eyes off Him, grab back the controls, and leave ourselves anxious and distracted.

This wavering faith is a burden to us. Will we ever learn to keep our eyes only on Jesus and not the circumstances?

January 20

> But if you do not forgive others, then your Father
> will not forgive your transgressions.
>
> —Matthew 6:15, NASB

When Peter asked Jesus how often he should forgive someone who sins against him, he asked, "Up to seven times?" The rabbis taught the people that they should forgive those who offended them up to three times. Peter knew the number 7 to be a number of completeness, something that is finished, as in the creation week in Genesis 1. So maybe he was trying to be generous or felt that he already knew Jesus's answer.

Imagine Peter's surprise when Jesus said, "No, not seven times but seventy times seven." He said the Kingdom of Heaven can be compared to a king who decided to bring his accounts up to date with servants who had borrowed money from him. One of them owed him millions of dollars. Since he couldn't pay such an amount, the master ordered that he be sold, along with his wife and children.

> But the man fell down before his master and begged him, "Please, be patient with me, and I will pay it all." The master pitied him, forgave his debt and released him. But when the man left the king, he went to a fellow servant who owed him a few thousand dollars and demanded instant payment.
>
> His fellow servant pleaded with him for a little more time. But he refused to wait, had the man arrested and put in prison.
>
> When some of the other servants saw this, they were very upset. They went to the king and told him everything that had happened. Then the king called in the man he had forgiven and said, "You evil servant! I forgave you that tremendous debt because you pleaded with me. Shouldn't you have mercy on your fellow servant, just as I had mercy on you?" Then the angry king sent the man to prison to be tortured until he had paid his entire debt.

That's what My heavenly Father will do to you if you refuse to forgive your brothers and sisters from your heart. (Matt. 18:26–35, NASB)

Seventy times seven! We shouldn't even keep track of how many times we forgive someone! Jesus often gave unexpected answers. When we think of this one, it calls for free and generous attitude of forgiveness.

Jesus, You have completely forgiven me. I am convinced that it is not within me to forgive as You command. Produce in me a free and generous attitude of forgiveness.

January 21

Sometimes I have such concern for friends and loved ones that I cannot verbalize my prayers for them. I am not a pessimist by nature, but after a disturbing phone call from one of them, I can sink from optimism to pessimism in a flash.

God's Word assures us that the Holy Spirit helps us in our weakness. When we don't know how to pray, the Holy Spirit prays for us with groanings that cannot be expressed in words.

And the Father, who knows all hearts, knows what the Spirit is saying, for the Spirit pleads for us in harmony with God's own will. He aligns us with

God's will when we are unable to do it on our own. (Rom. 8:26, NASB)

We don't have to say it or think it, for God knows our hearts! He knows the cry of our helplessness. He knows what the Spirit is saying as He pleads for us.

When we are in pain, sorrow, or deep concern for others, we can draw on the comfort of knowing that God didn't spare His only Son but gave Him up for us, and won't He also give us everything else?

We come before Him; words aren't necessary. We can rest on His promise.

January 22

> In everything give thanks; for this is
> God's will for you in Christ Jesus.
>
> —1 Thessalonians 5:18, NASB

How do we know God's will? We pray, "Your will be done." But what does that mean to us? Can we truly know what His will is for us?

I think of the decision to write this book. I wanted to, but having already written a devotional book, I knew how much time was involved.

I have read that when we want to know God's will, there are three things that always concur: the inward impulse, the Word of God, and the trend of circumstances! God in the heart, impelling you forward; God in the Book, corroborating whatever He said in the heart; and God in the circumstances, which are always indicative of His will.

I added one more to the mix: prayer. I start nothing without prayer. It is the switch to the power. With prayer came the inward impulse, and in time I began to jot down my thoughts.

Since God's Word is the book of choice when writing a daily devotional, I found myself immersed in the Book. Two of the three were in alignment.

And now, the circumstances came when I received a call from Tate Publishing asking if I would like to write another book! The final of the three—indicative of His will.

If you haven't tried this formula to understand God's will in your circumstances, try it. It will take patience and trust as you begin. I recommend you begin with prayer.

> Now to the King eternal, immortal,
> invisible, the only God, *be* honor and
> glory forever and ever. Amen.
>
> —1 Timothy 1:17, NASB

January 23

> For you were buried with Christ when you were
> baptized. And with Him you were raised to new
> life because you trusted the mighty power of God,
> who raised Christ from the dead.
>
> —Colossians 2:12, NLT

When circumstances press me and suffocate hope and trust, rescue me, Lord. Release me from all doubt; increase my faith.

Breathe Your Spirit deep into my soul. I long to be still before You, and yet distractions draw me away. My mind dwells on things that don't matter.

I find my heart steeped in sadness for those I know who are suffering.

I am anxious trying to meet commitments and deadlines. Be patient with me, Lord.

I turn to You, trusting You with loving confidence.

And when I do, all that cripples my spirit begins to dissipate.

I am victorious over hopelessness and misery.

I know You hear me, Lord. You love me and want the best for me.

And so I face this day knowing that You are with me. Praise You, Lord!

Lay your burdens on Him. It makes you light enough to help others carry theirs.

January 24

> But the very hairs of your head are all numbered.
>
> —Matthew 10:30, NKJV

My nine siblings and I have always had a full head of hair.

Not long ago I noticed some bald spots. I was diagnosed with alopecia areata, an autoimmune disorder. I have been getting cortisone shots in those spots, and for now at least, I have been able to control it, and I am grateful.

I think of this story:

> There once was a woman who woke up one morning, looked in the mirror, and noticed she had only three hairs on her head. "Well," she said, "I think I'll braid my hair today." So she did, and she had a wonderful day.
>
> The next day she woke up, looked in the mirror, and saw that she had only two hairs on her head. "Hmm," she said, "I think I'll part my hair down the middle today." So she did, and she had a grand day.
>
> The next day she woke up, looked in the mirror, and noticed that she had only one hair on her head.

"Well," she said, "today I'm going to wear my hair in a ponytail." So she did, and she had a fun, fun day.

The next day she woke up, looked in the mirror and noticed that there wasn't a single hair on her head. "Yeah!" she exclaimed, "I don't have to fix my hair today!"

Father, You are present in every aspect of our lives. We can face everything and anything knowing You are in control.

He has numbered the very hairs on our head. We are wonderfully made. Oh, that we may find every reason to thank Him, praising Him for His wonder and majesty. Full head of hair or no hair, we can always find a reason to have an attitude of gratitude.

January 25

One Sabbath day Jesus went to eat dinner in the home of a leader of the Pharisees.

When He noticed that all who had come to the dinner were trying to sit in the seats of honor near the head of the table, He gave them this advice:

> When you are invited by anyone to a wedding feast, do not sit down in the best place, lest one more

honorable than you be invited by him; and he who invited you and him come and say to you, "Give place to this man," and then you begin with shame to take the lowest place.

But when you are invited, go and sit down in the lowest place, so that when he who invited you comes he may say to you, "Friend, go up higher." Then you will have glory in the presence of those who sit at the table with you.

For whoever exalts himself will be humbled, and he who humbles himself will be exalted. (Luke 14:7–11, NKJV)

> Man shall not live by bread alone; but
> man lives by every *word* that proceeds
> from the mouth of the Lord.
>
> —Deuteronomy 8:3, NASB

January 26

> Love your neighbor as yourself.
>
> —Luke 10:27, NASB

A Jewish lawyer asked Jesus, "Who is my neighbor?"

> Jesus told him this story: "A man was on the road to Jericho when he was attacked by bandits. They stripped him, beat him and left him to die.
>
> A priest came along, and seeing the man, crossed to the other side.
>
> Likewise, when a Levite passed by and saw him, he did the same.
>
> A Samaritan saw the man, and filled with compassion, nursed him and took him to the inn and cared for him. The next day he gave the innkeeper two denarii and told him, 'Take care of him; and whatever more you spend, when I return I will repay you.'"
>
> Jesus asked the lawyer, "Which of these three do you think proved to be a neighbor to the man who fell into the robbers' hands?" He said, "The one who showed mercy toward him." Then Jesus said to him, "Go and do the same." (Luke 10:30–37, NASB)

There was deep hatred between the Jews and Samaritans. The lawyer felt the person least likely to help the man would be a Samaritan.

According to *Webster's* dictionary, compassion is a feeling of wanting to help someone who is sick, hungry, in trouble, etc.

It describes pity as a strong feeling of sadness or sympathy for someone or something. The priest and the Levite may have pitied the man, but they had no compassion for him.

It doesn't seem like it is such a leap between the two. Instead of pitying our neighbor who is sick, we can offer to mow his lawn.

Instead of pitying the single mom, we can offer to watch the children so she can spend some time by herself.

We look around and see a world in need of compassion. Feel and do! Love!

January 27

What an impact it would have on my life if I lived exclusively by faith! How freeing it would be to rely totally on You and Your promises.

You tell me to worry about nothing. Nothing! You feed the ravens; they don't plant or harvest, and they don't store up food. I am more valuable than them (Luke 12:24, NASB).

You clothe the lilies and the grass. They are here today, gone tomorrow. How much more will You clothe me! (Luke 12:27–28, NASB)

I want to live like the birds of the air and the lilies of the field. I want to soar; I want to blossom!

Worry cannot add a single hour to my life. I live by faith because You know what I need.

I will seek Your kingdom, and You will provide all I need.

Worry does not empty tomorrow of its sorrow, it empties today of its strength.

—Corrie ten Boom

January 28

Don't you realize that in a race everyone runs, but only one person gets the prize? So run to win! All athletes are disciplined in their training. They do it to win a prize that will fade away, but we do it for an eternal prize.

So I run with purpose in every step. I am not just shadowboxing. I discipline my body like an athlete, training it to do what it should. Otherwise, I fear that after preaching to others I myself might be disqualified. (1 Cor. 9:24–27, NLT)

I have fought the good fight, I have finished the race, I have kept the faith. Finally, there is laid up for me the crown of righteousness, which the Lord, the righteous Judge, will give to me on that Day, and not to me only but also to all who have loved His appearing. (2 Tim. 4:7–8, NKJV)

If you read history you will find that the Christians who did the most for the present world were precisely those who thought most of the next. It is since Christians have largely ceased to think of the other world that they have become so ineffective in this world.

—C. S. Lewis

January 29

As the rain and the snow come down from heaven, and do not return to it without watering the earth and making it bud and flourish, so that it yields seed for the sower and bread for the eater, so is My word that goes out from My mouth. It will not return to Me empty, but will accomplish what I desire and achieve the purpose for which I sent it.

—Isaiah 55:10–11, NLT

Our connection to the outside world has never been as widespread as it is today.

When God's Word is sent out, it always produces fruit. It will accomplish all that God wants it to, and it will prosper everywhere He sends it. We can be the instrument by which His Word is read.

When I send e-mails to a friend or loved one who is hurting, grieving, or struggling, I include a scripture verse with a clip art picture.

Paul writes that his life is worth nothing to him unless he uses it for finishing the work assigned by Jesus; the work of telling others the Good News about the wonderful grace of God (Acts 20:24, NLT).

I agree with Paul. Do you?

> Heaven and earth will disappear,
> but My words will never disappear.
>
> —Matthew 24:35, NLT

January 30

There are the times when I feel I have nothing meaningful to say to those I love who are enduring the battles of ill health.

I was comforted with this message sent by a friend when I had open heart surgery and a longer recovery than I had anticipated.

I needed the quiet, so He drew me aside into the shadows, where we could confide, away from the hustle, where all the day long I hurried and worried when active and strong.

I needed the quiet, though at first I rebelled, but gently, so gently my cross He upheld, and whispered so sweetly of spiritual things.

Though weakened in body, my spirit took wings to heights never dreamed of when active and gay.

He loved me so gently, He drew me away.

I needed the quiet, no prison my bed, but a beautiful valley of blessing instead,

a place to grow richer in Jesus to hide,

I needed the quiet so He drew me aside. (Unknown)

January 31

So why? Only God understands why we are allowed to suffer. Someday we will know. I think of Job and wonder how he could endure such testing and still say, "As for me, I know that my Redeemer lives" (Job 19:25, NASB).

Phillip Yancey calls this raw, naked faith. Although Job didn't have all the answers, he believed. "And it is impossible to please God without faith. Anyone who wants to come to Him must believe that God exists and that He rewards those who sincerely seek Him" (Heb. 11:6, NLT).

Maybe Job is planted in the scriptures so that we may be encouraged to know that although we do suffer, He never leaves us—our Rock! And by faith we know that He heals the brokenhearted and binds up our wounds.

We pray with groanings too deep for words and are grateful that He understands our shattered heart. Job's story gives us hope that just as God restored him, so He can restore us.

And with Job, we too can say that no matter what, "I know that my Redeemer lives."

> I have thanked Thee a thousand times for my roses, but not once for my thorn. I have been looking forward to a world where I shall get compensation for my cross, but I have never thought of my cross as itself a present glory. Thou Divine Love, whose human path has been perfected through sufferings, teach me the glory of my cross and the value of my thorn.
>
> —George Matheson

February 1

> Yet those who wait for the Lord
> will gain new strength.
>
> —Isaiah 40:31, NASB

I have made some bad judgment calls in my life, the consequences of which have been severe and far-reaching.

Life altering events could have left me crippled and unable to face the future. I traveled at a snail's pace through a recovery that seemed remote.

But I believe I have grown more sensitive to others who find themselves locked in limbo, dealing with the misery of mistakes.

I marvel at the wonder of the God who loves me most. He has pieced back together the broken fragments that lay untouched for so long. Scars have healed. Forgiveness is not something to be attained but an integral part of who I am. I learned to forgive.

Ruth Graham, in her book *In Every Pew Sits a Broken Heart,* writes, "I now understand that God was at work in my life all along. In my pain, in my suffering, in my mistakes—even in the dark—God was always present, working out His good purpose. Jesus is called Emmanuel, 'God with us'" (Matt. 1:23, KJV).

The redeeming grace for us is that God doesn't give up on us. When we feel like a failure, He is faithful. When we turn back to Him, He is there waiting for us to return. He doesn't scold us; He holds us. And herein lies our hope and future.

February 2

In the book of Philippians Paul nails the formula for a united family in spite of personality differences. He writes that unity is agreeing wholeheartedly with each other, loving one another, and working together with one mind and purpose.

These are high standards to achieve. But he tells how to accomplish that: don't be selfish or conceited. With humility, regard one another as more important than yourself, and don't merely look out for your own personal interests but also for the interests of everyone. We must have the same attitude that Christ Jesus had (Phil. 2:3–5, NASB).

Desmond Tutu, in *An Invitation to Forgive*, writes, "In my own family, sibling squabbles have spilled into inter-generational alienations. When adult siblings refuse to speak to each other because of some offense, recent or long past, their children and grandchildren can lose out on the joy of strong family relationships. The children and grand-children may never know what occasioned the freeze. They know only that 'We don't visit this aunt' or 'We don't really know those cousins.' Forgiveness among the members of older generations will open the door to healthy and supportive relationships among younger generations. Are we willing to let go of differences and strive to achieve unity?"

Families are sometimes fragmented and fragile. One member who is disengaged can cripple the strength of unity. I don't want to be the one, do you?

February 3

Father, I know You don't jump in to answer my every request. But You cause everything to work together for my good because I love You and am called according to Your purpose. You have predetermined that I am to become conformed to the image of Your Son, Jesus. You know in advance what I need.

You call me to come to You, and You will give me right standing with You. What a wonderful thing!

If You are for me, who can ever be against me? You didn't spare even Your own Son but gave Him up for me! How will You not give me everything that I need?

Nothing can ever separate me from Your love. I will never doubt that. No matter what troubles me, what sorrow or tragedy befall me, nothing will separate me from You. Victory is mine through You (Rom. 8:28–31, 39, NLT).

February 4

> He will wipe every tear from their eyes, and there
> will be no more death or sorrow or crying or pain.
> All these things are gone forever.
>
> —Revelation 21:4, NLT

When my three-year-old granddaughter Jessica died, it was a two-edged sword for me. There was the cutting helplessness I felt watching my son gripped with grief and searching for anything to numb the pain.

The other edge was my wavering between disbelief and questioning. Jessica's death threw me to my knees. I fell before God questioning *why?* I didn't blame Him, but I felt He had allowed it.

I believe her death was the catalyst that brought me to this intimate relationship with God. He listened to my question and replaced it with the answer—Him!

Death will come to us all. Those we leave behind will suffer the agonizing journey to carry on. And I know now that only by Him, through Him, and with Him are we able to slowly pick ourselves back up and walk from the darkness into the sunlight.

Grief never ends.
It changes.
Grief is a passage not a place to stay.
It's not a sign of weakness or lack of faith.
It's the price of love. (Unknown)

February 5

Your faithful love never ends; Your mercies never cease; they are fresh each morning. My heart rejoices, for great is Your faithfulness.

You have set my feet on solid ground and steady me as I walk along.

You have given me a new song to sing—a hymn of praise.

I find such joy when trusting in You.

O Lord, You have performed many wonders in my life.

Your plans for me are too numerous to list.

You have no equal.

If I tried to recite all of Your wonderful deeds, I would never come to the end of them.

My confidence is in You as I experience Your promises.

Thank You, Jesus!

February 6

> You make known to me the path of life; You will
> fill me with joy in Your presence, with eternal
> pleasures at Your right hand.
>
> —Psalm 16:11, NLT

We were created for God's pleasure. In these closing moments of this age, the Lord will have a people whose purpose for living is to please God with their lives.

In them, God finds His own reward for creating man. They are His worshipers. They are on earth only to please God, and when He is pleased, they also are pleased.

The Lord takes them farther and through more pain and conflicts than other men. Outwardly, they often seem "smitten of God, and afflicted," yet to God, they are His beloved. When they are crushed, like the petals of a flower, they exude a worship, the fragrance of which is so beautiful and rare that angels weep in quiet awe at their surrender. They are the Lord's purpose for creation. (Francis Frangipane)

When you and I hurt deeply, what we really need is not an explanation from God but a revelation of

God. We need to see how great God is; we need to recover our lost perspective on life. Things get out of proportion when we are suffering, and it takes a vision of something bigger than ourselves to get life's dimensions adjusted again. (Warren W. Wiersbe)

February 7

Lord, You are mine! I belong to You. I relish this truth, and I long for Your blessings and mercy.

I think about the direction of my life, and I promise I will obey Your words.

The world knows of my love and faithfulness to You, and it persistently tries to lure me away.

There was a time I succumbed and wandered off. Your discipline drew me back and taught me to pay attention to Your words, which are now more valuable to me than gold and silver.

Surround me with Your tender mercies so that I may live according to Your instructions. You are my God, and I place my life in Your hands.

You promise me that You will never let me go, that You will honor me by anointing my head with oil. My cup runs over!

February 8

Child, don't just pretend to love others, really love them with genuine affection.

Hate what is wrong and hold tightly to what is good.

When you see others in need, be ready to help them.

There will always be those who hurt you, sometimes by their words and sometimes by their actions toward you. Bless them, and you will be blessed.

Be happy with those who are happy, and weep with those who weep.

Live in harmony and peace with each other.

When someone is hungry, feed them. And if they are thirsty, give them something to drink.

Please remember I am always with you to strengthen and encourage you. When you love Me with all your heart and soul, loving others will follow (Rom. 12:9–16, NLT).

February 9

I can do everything through You because You give me strength.

You are the Creator of everything in heaven and on earth.

Your glorious unlimited resources empower me with inner strength through Your Spirit.

When I wait on You, I will find new strength in You each moment of this day.

I will soar on wings like eagles. I will run and not get tired, and I will walk and not get weary (Isa. 40:31, NASB).

Circumstances will not weigh me down. Your grace is all I need, for Your power works best in me when I am weak.

No matter what the day may bring, I will rejoice in You!

February 10

> Those who live in the shelter of the Most High
> will find rest in the shadow of the Almighty.
>
> —Psalm 91:1, NLT

I cannot help the thought, which grows steadily upon me, that the better part of prayer is not the asking but the kneeling where we can ask, the resting there, and staying there, drawing out the willing moments in heavenly communion with God within the closet.

Just to be there at leisure from ourselves, at leisure from the world, with our souls at liberty, with our spirit feeling its kinship to the Divine Spirit, with our life finding itself in the life of God—this is prayer.

Would it be possible that one could be thus with God, listening to Him, speaking to Him, reposing upon His love, and not come out with a shining face, a gladdened heart, and intent more constant and more strong to give to the waiting world, which so sadly needs it, what has been taken from the heart of God?[2]

February 11

> And why worry about a speck in your friend's eye
> when you have a log in your own? How can you
> think of saying to your friend, 'Let me help you get
> rid of that speck in your eye,' when you can't see
> past the log in your own eye?
>
> —Matthew 7:3–4, NLT

O Lord, despite my repeated efforts, I found myself at odds with her—a damaged relationship. I am human and couldn't resolve the conflict between love and forgiveness. Ever so gently You spoke to me through Your Word:

Child, don't judge others, and you won't be judged. You will be treated with the same standard as you treat others.

Why do you worry about the speck in her eye? I can see the log in yours. Can you honestly tell her that you will help her get rid of the speck when you deny there is a log in your eye?

Let Me help you remove the log and provide you flawless vision that will clear the way to a restored relationship. Come to Me.

Jesus says to cast your burdens on Him. Is your heaviest burden *you*? Cast!

February 12

Child, don't store up treasures here on earth, where moths eat them and rust destroys them, and where thieves break in and steal. Store your treasures in heaven, where moths and rust cannot destroy, and thieves do not break in and steal.

Wherever your treasure is, there the desires of your heart will also be.

Your eye is a lamp that provides light for your body. When your eye is good, your whole body is filled with light. But when your eye is bad, your whole body is filled with darkness. No one can serve two masters. For you will hate one and love the other; you will be devoted to one and despise the other. You cannot serve both Me and money (Matt. 6:19–24, NLT).

> Teach me Thy love to know;
> That this new light which now I see,

May both the work and workman show.
Then by a sunbeam I will climb to Thee. (George Herbert)

February 13

> Now may the God of peace—who brought up
> from the dead our Lord Jesus, the great Shepherd
> of the sheep, and ratified an eternal covenant
> with His blood—may He equip you with all you
> need for doing His will. May He produce in you,
> through the power of Jesus Christ, every good
> thing that is pleasing to Him. All glory to Him
> forever and ever! Amen
>
> —Hebrews 13:20–21, NLT

Equip me, Lord, with all I need for doing Your will. I make my plans, but I hold them loosely. With You as the center of my planning, You will guide me.

If my plans are suddenly altered, I will not be anxious, for I can trust You in all circumstances.

God of Peace, through Your power, produce in me every good thing that is pleasing to You.

> Thy will, not mine, O Lord,
> However dark it be!

Lead me by Thine own hand,
Choose out the path for me.
I dare not choose my lot;
I would not if I might.
Choose Thou for me, My God
So shall I walk aright. (Horatius Bonar)

February 14

Child, be strong in Me and in My power. Put on your armor so that you will be able to stand firm against the strategies of the devil. You are not fighting against flesh-and-blood enemies but against the power of an unseen and dark world.

Don every piece of My armor so you can resist the enemy and still be standing firm after the battle.

Put on the belt of truth, and the body armor of My righteousness

Your shoes are the peace that comes from the Good News, which will fully prepare you.

Your shield of faith stops the arrows of the devil.

Your helmet is salvation.

Always carry the sword of the Spirit, which is My Word

Pray at all times, staying alert and persistent in prayer for the family of believers everywhere (Eph. 6:10–19, NLT).

The sword is My powerful and mighty Word. This is your only offensive weapon. The rest of the armor are defensive weapons. Don't forget to keep your sword sharpened!

February 15

For several months after my daughter graduated high school and left to join her sister about three hours away, I could still hear the familiar sound of the Pontiac turning the corner into the driveway. "Hi, Mom!" In my head, I heard her voice as she opened the door.

I was experiencing the empty-nest syndrome. It was major! Eighteen years of nurturing, and in one day she had moved away. Could anyone understand how I felt?

I busied myself with the routine of volunteering and serving in my women's ministry. But still it was quiet and lonely.

Gradually those sounds dimmed, and the phone was my connection to her new world, one that was exciting and fulfilling for her.

God understands the emotional transitions that come to us all.

- I prayed to the Lord and He answered me. He freed me from all my fears (Ps. 34:4, NLT).
- Taste and see that the Lord is good. Oh, the joys of those who take refuge in Him! (Ps. 34:8, NLT)

- The eyes of the Lord watch over those who do right; His ears are open to their cries for help (Ps. 34:15, NLT).
- The Lord is close to the brokenhearted; He rescues those whose spirits are crushed (Ps. 34:18, NLT).

February 16

> There are different kinds of spiritual gifts, but the same Spirit is the source of them all.
>
> —1 Corinthians 12:4, NLT

A spiritual gift is given to us so we can help each other. It is the Spirit who distributes all these gifts and decides which gift each person should have.

Heavenly Father, help me to fan the flames of the spiritual gifts You have given me. I know You have not given me a spirit of fear and timidity but of power, love, and a sound mind. These are unyielding tools by which I am able to serve You. They give me the accessibility to employ the works You have set within me.

You have called me to live a holy life, insufficient and undeserving as I am. But You have a plan for me. By Your grace and through Your Son, Jesus, who shattered the power of death over me, You have illuminated the way for me to live a holy life.

Help me to recognize my special gifts, and instill in me a burning desire to use them for Your honor and glory.

February 17

> Consider it pure joy, my brothers and sisters
> whenever you face trials of many kinds, because
> you know that the testing of your faith produces
> perseverance. Let perseverance finish its work
> so that you may be mature and complete, not
> lacking anything.
>
> —James 1:2–4, NLT

Joni Eareckson Tada was seventeen when she dove into a river, was seriously injured, and became a quadriplegic.

She says, "My affliction has stretched my hope, made me know Christ better, helped me long for truth, led me to repentance of sin, goaded me to give thanks in times of sorrow, increased my faith, and strengthened my character. Being in this wheelchair has meant knowing Him better, feeling His pleasure every day."

Many of her reflections came years after the accident, having endured the agony of permanent disability and life changes.

Jesus, when troubles come my way, I pray I can consider them an opportunity for great joy. May I know that when my faith is tested, my endurance will have a chance to grow. And when my endurance is fully developed, I will be perfect and complete, needing nothing.

February 18

> I long to dwell in Your tent forever and take refuge
> in the shelter of Your wings.
>
> —Psalm 61:4, NLT

I admit I don't feel very close to You right now. I am feeling helpless about the challenges swirling around me. I don't know how or what to pray anymore. Rid me of worry. Lift me up to Your eternal presence, where I can rest in You. Then return to the things I need to do, meeting each one free from concern.

I feel helpless but not hopeless, for my hope is in You. You are my help.

Child, here under My wing, nothing harmful can find you. Nestle in, and I will allow nothing to disturb you. You are safe and protected, free from all care.

Don't be afraid, for I am with you. Don't be discouraged, for I am your God

I will strengthen you and help you. I will hold you up with My victorious right hand (Isa. 41:10, NLT).

If you are overcome with fear and worry, return here, and I will cover you. Rest here under My wing. Do you feel the warmth of My love?

> Commit yourself wholeheartedly
> to these words of Mine.
>
> —Deuteronomy 11:18, NLT

February 19

> We have waited for You. Be our strong arm each
> day and our salvation in times of trouble.
>
> —Isaiah 33:2, NLT

Thank You for Your promise of the joy I will know when You return. But I know for now there are trials ahead, some so fierce they will test my faith as fire purifies gold. I need Your power to remain strong, so that my perseverance, because of my faith, will bring You honor and glory.

I trust You as I wait for the day of Your return.

I don't look forward to what lies ahead in this vale of tears, but my heart leaps with joy to what awaits me when I see You face to face. My reward will be the salvation of my soul.

God is my strong salvation,
What foe have I to fear?
In darkness and temptation,
My Light, my Help is near.
Though hosts encamp around me,
Firm to the fight I stand,
What terror can confound me
With God at my right hand? (James Montgomery)

February 20

> Come, let us return to the Lord, for He has torn
> us, but He will heal us, He has wounded us, but
> He will bandage us.
>
> —Hosea 6:1, NASB

God had allowed His beloved people to be held captive by the Babylonians for seventy years because they had rejected and disobeyed Him. But He assured them if they would turn to Him, repent, and seek Him, He would welcome them.

I cling to God's promise that when we return to Him, He will heal us. I have been torn and wounded by some of the events of my life. Those times that I have done things my own way, I was taken captive by the world and held in slavery by what it offered.

There was no one moment that I can remember when I returned to Him. It was a gradual process, one of mistakes and severe consequences. But I did return. He has welcomed me as His precious child and bandaged my wounds. I was torn, but now I am healed.

It is never too late for us to turn to Him. God longs for a relationship with each of us.

I like the saying, "Life can only be understood backward, but it must be lived forward."

February 21

> He will be gracious if you ask for help. He will
> surely respond to the sound of your cries.
>
> —Isaiah 30:19, NLT

Oh, yes! I am brought to tears by Your wondrous love for me. I call upon You, and You answer me. You work in me through Your Word.

Nothing is accomplished in my life unless You are the center of my every thought, motivation, and reason. All else I consider as failure. Here I am again with wordless adoration for the kindness You have shown.

You don't wave a magic wand and make things happen. You work slowly, leading me with gentle guidance in the way that I should go.

You don't push or pull but instead tell me to wait on Your counsel—to be still.

I am listening.

> How sweet Your words taste to me; they are
> sweeter than honey.
>
> —Psalm 119:103, NLT

February 22

Ponderings:

- "When a train goes through a tunnel and it gets dark, you don't throw away the ticket and jump off. You sit still and trust the engineer" (Corrie Ten Boom).
- "Patience is not passive; on the contrary, it is active, it is concentrated strength" (E. G. Bulver-Lyton).
- "Every heart has a secret sorrow" (Henry Longfellow).
- "Courage is fear holding on a minute longer" (George S. Patton).
- "To dream of the person you would like to be is to waste the person you are" (Anonymous).
- "People are like stained-glass windows. They sparkle and shine when the sun is out, but when the darkness

sets in, their true beauty is revealed only if their light is from within" (Winston Churchill).

- "Mere information makes no one righteous, it only makes us responsible for what we know. The degree to which we know something is the degree to which we have integrated it into our lives" (C. S. Lewis).

February 23

> Through suffering, our bodies continue to share in
> the death of Jesus so that the life of Jesus may also
> be seen in our bodies.
>
> —2 Corinthians 4:10, NLT

Child, I am the Light in the darkness. Satan, who is the god of this world, has blinded the minds of those who don't believe in Me. They are unable to see the glorious light of the Good News.

You are like a fragile clay pot containing this great treasure. It is My power, not yours, which shines.

This power helps you endure troubles that attack you on every side, but they won't crush you. Don't despair, for I will never abandon you. It is by trial and suffering that My powerful light will shine through you so that all who see you will know I am the Light in the darkness.

You can meet the future confident of My protection. You are armored with My grace for whatever comes your way.

Do not allow fear or anxiety to dictate your life. Pause in those moments; recenter yourself and find My divine grace replacing those moments with My peace.

> All of us have wondered at times why God doesn't do more to fix our problems. But our human eyes often fail to see that God isn't rushing to change our circumstances because he is concerned with a much more serious problem—our character. While you struggle with the woes of this world, God's main occupation is preparing you for the world to come. The focus of what God is doing in your life takes place in you, not around you.
>
> —Andy Stanley

February 24

O God, I long to know You more intimately through Your Word and to listen to You in every aspect of my life.

Help me to resist the things of this world.

Purify my heart!

Help me to know and do Your will without ceasing in spite of any inclination to do things my way. I listen, O Lord. I long to know what You would have me do.

> I ask not that my course be calm and still;
> no, here too, Lord, be done Thy holy will.
> I ask but for a quiet childlike heart.
> Though thronging cares and restless toil be mine,
> yet may my heart remain forever Thine;
> draw it from earth and fix it where Thou art. (C. J.
>   P. Spitta)

February 25

Give me strength to live another day;
Let me not turn coward before its difficulties or prove recreant to its duties;
Let me not lose faith in other people;
Keep me sweet and sound of heart, in spite of ingratitude, treachery or meanness;
Preserve me from minding little stings or giving them;
Help me to keep my heart clean and to live so honestly and fearlessly that no outward failure can dishearten me or take away the joy of conscious integrity;
Open wide the eyes of my soul that I may see good in all things;

Grant me this day some new vision of Thy truth;
Inspire me with a spirit of joy and gladness;
and make me the cup of strength to suffering souls;
in the name of the strong Deliverer, our only Lord and
Savior, Jesus Christ. Amen.[3]

February 26

Child, when the earthly tent in which you are living is taken down (when you die) you will have a home in heaven. You will have an eternal body made for you by Me, your God.

I know you grow weary in your present body and long to put on your heavenly body like new clothing. You will not be a spirit without a body, for I will give you a heavenly body in which to live. That is beyond your comprehension, isn't it?

In your present body, you groan and sigh. It's not that you are anxious to die, but you await with anticipation for the promise of a new body. I will continue to prepare you for this transition (2 Cor. 5:1–5, NLT).

So always be confident; live by believing in Me, and not in things that can't be seen. For what you see now will soon be gone, but the things you cannot see will last forever.

Fix your gaze on Me.

Though your body is dying, your spirit is being renewed every day by the Holy Spirit.

Your Word is a lamp for my feet,
a light on my path.

—Psalm 119:105, NLT

February 27

What would our life be like if we abandoned all of ourselves into the hands of the Lord?

Take, O Lord, and receive all my memory, my
understanding and my will.
All that I have and posses Thou hast given to me;
to Thee O Lord I restore it.
All is Thine; dispose of it according to Your Will.
Give me Thy love and Thy grace for that is enough
for me.

—Ignatius Loyola

There is a persuasion in the soul of man that he is
here for cause; that he was put in this place by the
Creator to do the work for which He inspires him.

—Ralph Waldo Emerson

February 28

If you've ever lugged a heavy suitcase through the airport, you understand baggage! I always pack more than I need. I would rather be like the younger passengers: a backpack tossed into the overhead bin.

Baggage—we carry more than is necessary. We slump under the weight of guilt, unforgiveness, resentment, blame—the emotions we pack and carry. It's foolish!

I've carried an overload of those burdens, mostly guilt for things I did and things I didn't do. I tucked them away so that I could get on with my life. I didn't have time to deal with such things. But reminders kept cropping up, and each time I packed them away, my load getting heavier.

I started full-time into women's Bible studies. Over time without realizing it, buried shame of the past began to dissolve. Only by dropping the soul-breaking load at the feet of Jesus was I able to relieve myself of the weight. There I learned that I needed first to forgive myself. That was a daunting task, one that I didn't want to undertake.

It was a slow process. But the Holy Spirit guided me through scriptures that allowed me to forgive myself as God had forgiven me. The Word of God was cleansing me of all past mistakes.

- I—yes, I alone—will blot out your sins for My own sake and will never think of them again (Isa. 43:25, NLT).
- Though your sins are like scarlet, I will make them as white as snow. Though they are red like crimson, I will make them as white as wool (Isa. 1:18, NLT).
- As far as the east is from the west, so far has He removed our transgressions from us (Ps. 103:12, NLT).
- Come to me, all of you who are weary and carry heavy burdens, and I will give you rest (Matt. 11:28, NLT).

I started unpacking! I now have a light backpack that I can throw in the overhead bin!

February 29

Because of what You have done for me, I have been made right in Your sight, and I have peace.

Praise You!

Because of my faith, You have brought me into this place of undeserved privilege where I stand. With confidence and joy, I look forward to sharing Your glory.

Praise You!

I know I can rejoice when I run into problems and trials because I know they help me develop endurance.

And endurance develops my strength of character.

And my character strengthens my confident hope of salvation. This hope will not lead to disappointment (Rom. 5:1–5, NLT).

You supply all I need.

Praise You!

There is nothing I have done that could bring me into fellowship with You. All that I have, all that I am is because of Your love for me. Why would You suffer and die on the cross for one so unworthy? It is a love I cannot comprehend.

Praise You!

Your grace enables me to live as You want me to live, and You have given me the Holy Spirit to fill my heart with Your love.

Praise You!

March 1

> If you love Me, keep My commands.
>
> —John 14:15, NKJV

Jesus's work on earth was about to be finished; it would be time for Him to join the Father. He knew those who loved and followed Him would mourn, and He wanted to assure them that He would not leave them without a Helper.

He told them that the Father would give them another Advocate to help them and be with them forever—the Spirit of truth.

He said, "The Helper, the Holy Spirit, whom the Father will send in My name, will teach you all things, and bring to your remembrance all things that I said to you. Peace I leave with you, My peace I give to you; not as the world gives do I give to you. Let not your heart be troubled, neither let it be afraid."

> When He, the Spirit of truth, has come, He will guide you into all truth; for He will not speak on His own *authority*, but whatever He hears He will speak; and He will tell you things to come. He will glorify Me, for He will take of what is Mine and declare *it* to you. (John 16:13–14, NKJV)

Jesus, my time here with You is the best part of my day. You fill me with overwhelming gratitude, and I rejoice as the Holy Spirit moves in the quiet of my soul, stirring me to love You more. You are more than I can ever know in this life. But someday I will be in Your presence face-to-face, and we can talk!

March 2

> He loves whatever is just and good;
> the unfailing love of the Lord fills the earth.
>
> —Psalm 33:5, NLT

Nothing can compare to You, Almighty God!
You merely spoke,
and the heavens were created.
You breathed the word,
and all the stars were born.
You assigned the sea its boundaries
and locked the oceans in vast reservoirs.
The whole world shall fear You,
and stand in awe of You.
For when You spoke, the world began!
It appeared at Your command.
You frustrate the plans of the nations
and thwart all their schemes.
But Your plans, O LORD, stand firm forever;
Your intentions can never be shaken (Ps. 33:6–11).

March 3

> But we don't need to write to you about the
> importance of loving each other, for God Himself
> has taught you to love one another.
>
> —1 Thessalonians 4:9, NLT

This is the great business and meaning of our life on earth: that we should more and more yield up our hearts to God's great grace of love. And that we should let it enter ever more fully and more freely into us so that it may even fill our whole heart and life.

We must day after day be driving back, in His strength, the sin that doth so easily beset us and the selfishness that sin has fastened in our hearts; and then His love will day by day increase in us.

Prayer will win and keep it; work will strengthen and exercise it; the Bible will teach us how to know and prize it, how to praise God for it; the Holy Eucharist will ever renew and quicken its power in our hearts.

And so (blessed be God!) love and joy and peace will grow in us, beyond all that we can ask or think, and He will forgive us, for love's sake, all the failures, all the faults in whatever work He has given us to do, and will bring us at last into the fullness of that life which even here He has suffered us to know—into that one Eternal Home, where love is perfect and unwearied and unending and where nothing ever can part us from one another or from Him. [4]

March 4

What is prayer to you? Volumes have been written about the subject.

As I mature spiritually, I am led to a deeper desire to know God personally by talking with Him.

That is *my* simple definition of prayer: talking personally to God. I am in constant conversation with Him. He abides in me, and I converse with Him more often than any other person I know.

Before this intimate relationship began to grow, I took for granted the slightest evidence of His presence. Now I am spiritually aware and thank Him for even the smallest blessings. I seek Him in every endeavor, no matter how minute it may seem, with a heartfelt desire that it accomplish His will in my life.

Maybe like me you never thought about having a personal relationship with Jesus. It makes me think of something He has said. He said, "I stand at the door and knock. If you hear My voice, open the door and invite Me in, I will come in and dine with you" (Rev. 3:20).

Dine with you! This is an image denoting intimacy and friendship. In all countries and times, to eat together has been the symbol of friendship, and that is what He promises here. He uses this metaphor to indicate the measures He will take to have a personal relationship with us.

Whatever prayer is to us, God will honor every glance of our heart toward Him. He alone knows what is in our heart. Praise Him for the intimacy that only you and He share. To Him be all glory and honor forever and ever. Amen!

March 5

> Don't sin by letting anger control you. Don't let
> the sun go down while you are still angry, for anger
> gives foothold to the devil.
>
> —Ephesians 4:26, NLT

We all deal with anger. In the Greek language it is defined as the strongest of passions. Anger can be fueled by injustice, impatience, abuse, unmet needs, jealousy, and more. In many situations anger masks feelings of grief, loneliness, and hurt feelings. It is a defense mechanism to avoid emotions we don't understand.

I think of the time as a teenager when I was to be home by dark. I wasn't. My dad met me while I was approaching. He was angry! Only when I became a parent myself did I understand that his anger was a response to fear of what might have happened to me.

Controlling anger can begin when we recognize the underlying cause. There is a difference between getting angry and being an angry person. No matter what the cause of anger might be, God's Word says anger is sin when we let it control us.

And if we end our day without having dealt with it, we give Satan a stronger grip to control us. Anger has a way of building a stockpile in our hearts. The builder is Satan. We must not give him any material that will give him a firm footing in our relationship with God.

> Be quick to listen, slow to speak,
> and slow to get angry
>
> —James 1:19, NASB

March 6

> Now may our Lord Jesus Christ Himself
> and God our Father, who loved us and by
> His grace gave us eternal comfort and a
> wonderful hope, comfort you and strengthen
> you in every good thing you do and say.
>
> —2 Thessalonians 2:16–17, NLT

All praise to You, O God, Father of my Lord Jesus Christ.

You are my merciful Father and the source of comfort in my troubles.

When I am crushed and overwhelmed, You touch me with compassion; I feel Your presence.

You fill me with joy when I can find none.

When I trust in You, You keep me in perfect peace.

Even though my health might fail, You remain my Healer. You tend to my needs, embracing my weakened body.

Why would I not rely totally on You? You who brought the dead to life. And when my spirit appears as though dead, I rush to You, placing my confidence in You, that You will revive me.

Father, You shower me with Your comfort, and by Your grace, I will comfort others with the same comfort You have given me.

March 7

God knows very well what we need, and that all He does is for our good. If we knew how much He loves us, we would always be ready to face life—both its pleasures and its troubles.

Although we seek and love God because of the blessings He has given us or for those He may give us in the future, let us not stop there. These blessings, as great as they are, will never carry us as near to Him as a simple act of faith does in a time of need or trouble. Let us look to God with these eyes of faith. He is within us, and we don't need to seek Him elsewhere. We have only ourselves to blame if we turn from God, occupying ourselves instead with the trifles of life.

In the Lord's patience, He endures our weaknesses. But just think of the price we pay by being separated from His presence! Once and for all let us begin to be His entirely. Let us banish from our heart and soul all that does not reflect Jesus. Let us ask Him for the grace to do this, so that He alone might rule in our hearts.

I must confide in you, my dear friend, that I hope, in His grace, that I will see Him in a few days. Let us pray to Him for one another.[5]

(Brother Lawrence passed from this life into the next just a few days after writing this on February 12, 1691, to dwell fully in the presence of his God.)

March 8

I pray my love will overflow more and more, and I will grow in knowledge and understanding.

Help me know what really matters so that I may live a pure and blameless life until Your return.

Fill me with the fruit of Your salvation, and produce in me a righteous character. I ask this so that my obedient love for You will bring You honor and glory.

Child, draw close to Me, and I will draw close to You. I am as close to you as your next breath. Do you need to tell your body to breathe? No. And you need not tell Me of your longing.

Draw close, and My nearness will meet your every desire, your every need. You will be filled with the fruits of the Spirit. You will be made righteous through Me.

> Yes, take my heart, and in it rule;
> Direct it as it pleaseth Thee;
> I will be silent in Thy school,
> And learn what'er Thou teachest me. (Unknown)

March 9

> I know all the things you do, that you are neither
> hot nor cold. I wish that you were one or the other!
> But since you are like lukewarm water, neither hot
> nor cold, I will spit you out of My mouth!
>
> —Revelation 3:15–16, NLT

These words are written to the church in Laodicea, a fairly wealthy banking center and a textile town. The Laodiceans understood the analogy between hot and cold water because their city drinking water came from a spring six miles to the south over an aqueduct, and it arrived disgustingly lukewarm. It was not hot like the nearby hot springs that people bathed in, nor was it refreshingly cold for drinking. It was lukewarm—good for nothing. And they didn't have ice cubes!

Lukewarm is comfortable Christianity. One who is neither spiritually on fire for God nor cold, rejecting Him altogether. It is one who feels secure because they attend church, were baptized, and come from a Christian family. One who gives money to charity and the church as long as fits into the budget.

A comfortable Christian can look good on the outside, but God knows a hot or cold heart. "Hypocrites! For you are like whitewashed tombs which on the outside appear beautiful, but inside they are full of dead men's bones and all uncleanness" (Matt. 23:27, NASB).

These are convicting words! But a compassionate Christ goes on to say, "I correct and discipline everyone I love; so be diligent and turn from your indifference" (Rev. 3:19, NASB).

Even though Laodicea was lukewarm at this time, Jesus says that He still loves them; that is why He rebukes them. And He gives them counsel to turn away from their lukewarm lifestyle.

We stand at the sink and can turn on the hot or cold water. Combined, we get lukewarm. Which faucet will we turn on? Combined and comfortable? Hot or cold?

March 10

> "I know the plans I have for you," says the LORD.
> "They are plans for good and not for disaster, to
> give you a future and a hope."
>
> —Jeremiah 29:11, NLT

I begin this day anew centered in You, Lord Jesus.

It is quite true that to live a godly life is not an easy matter, but I experience Your deep love for me, and partake in Your wondrous gifts. I am lifted above the temptations offered by the world. I can rejoice when I run into problems and trials, for I know they are meant for good; they teach me patience.

Trusting You in all things, major and minor, develops strength of character, and my hope and faith stay steady and strong. When this happens, I know that all is well—that You are in control. This confidence springs within because I know of Your mercy and tenderness toward me. I can live a godly life through Your power and grace.

Child, I know the plans I have for You: plans for good, not for evil. They may not be the plans you would make for yourself; neither are my thoughts the same as yours. Just as the heavens are higher than the earth, so My ways are higher than yours and My thoughts than yours. Trust Me this day that you will know the full measure of My love and care for you.

All is well.

March 11

O LORD, my Lord,
How majestic is Your name in all the earth,
When I consider Your heavens, the work of Your
    fingers,
The moon and the stars, which You have ordained;
What am I that You take thought of me,
And the son of man that You care for me?
Yet You have made me a little lower than God,
And You crown me with glory and majesty!
You make me to rule over the works of Your hands;
You have put all things under my feet,
The beasts of the field, the birds of the heavens and
    the fish of the sea,
Whatever passes through the paths of the seas.
O LORD, my Lord, how majestic is Your name in all
    the earth! (Ps. 8:1–9, NLT)

I believe in Christianity in the same way as I
believe that the sun has risen. Not because I see *it*,
    but that by it, I see *everything* else.

—C. S. Lewis

March 12

Child, nothing positive is ever accomplished by complaining or arguing. Has anything that you desired to change, brought positive results by complaining? Whose mind have you changed by arguing? Imitate Me in all that you do.

When throngs, eager for My attention, left Me tired and weary, I didn't complain.

When challenged by those would have Me killed, I wasn't drawn into arguing. I said what was true and right. It was up to them to reject it or accept it.

I didn't retaliate when I was insulted nor threaten revenge when I suffered. I left this in the hands of My Father, who always judges fairly.

I call you to live as a bright light in this world. This light within you produces what is good, right, and true.

And those whose intention is to argue and complain will be exposed when the light shines on them, for the light makes everything visible. Live your life following My example. You will reap the benefits of peace and serenity.

> Set a guard, O Lord, over my mouth;
> keep watch over the door of my lips.
>
> —Psalm 141:3, NASB

March 13

Lord, You are mine! I promise to obey Your words!

With all my heart I want Your blessings. Be merciful as You promised.

I ponder the direction of my life, and I turn to follow Your laws. I will hurry without delay to obey You.

The world tries to drag me into sin, but I am firmly anchored to what You want me to do. Even during the night I wake to thank You.

I am a friend to anyone who fears You—anyone who follows You.

O Lord, Your unfailing love fills the earth; teach me Your decrees.

You have done many good things for me, Lord, just as You promised.

I believe in Your commands; teach me good judgment and knowledge.

In the past I have wandered off, but You have disciplined me. Now I closely follow Your Word.

You are good and do only good. I know that I belong to You.

It is a great thing to see physical courage, and
greater still to see moral courage, but the greatest

to see of all is spiritual courage; oh, to see a person
who will stand true to the integrity of Jesus Christ
no matter what he or she goes through!

—Oswald Chambers

March 14

Child, in this life there will be suffering and death. But
though your eyes fail from weeping and you feel dis-
tressed, My great love will not allow you to be consumed by trouble, for My compassions never fail.
They are new every morning; great is My faithfulness.
I will be good to you because you hope in Me; you continue to seek Me. It is good for you to wait quietly for
My salvation.

If you want to be My disciple, you must deny yourself,
take up your cross, and follow Me.

If you want to save your life, you will lose it, but if you
lose your life for Me, you will find it. What good will it
be for you to gain the whole world, yet forfeit your soul?
Or what can you give in exchange for your soul? (Matt.
16:24–26, NASB)

I am the Resurrection and the Life; he who believes in
Me will live even if he dies, and everyone who lives and

believes in Me will never die. Do you believe this? (John 11:25–26, NASB)

> The grass withers and the flowers fade, but the
> Word of our God stands forever.
>
> —Isaiah 40:8, NLT

March 15

> When Joseph's brothers saw him coming, they
> recognized him in the distance. As he approached,
> they made plans to kill him.
>
> —Genesis 37:18, NLT

For me, besides the words "Forgive them, Father," from our suffering Savior, Joseph's forgiveness of his brothers is probably the most compelling example of forgiveness in the Bible.

His ten older brothers hated him because he was their father's favorite. They conspired to get rid of him and sold him into slavery for twenty shekels of silver. He was carted off to Egypt.

There he became a servant, was accused of rape, and thrown into prison. The king had a very disturbing dream, and Joseph's guards told the king that Joseph could interpret it for him. When he did, he was made ruler of Egypt, second only to the king.

Famine became catastrophic over the earth, and Joseph's brothers were sent by their father to Egypt to buy grain.

When the brothers realized who Joseph was, they feared for their lives. Surely He would retaliate! "Don't grieve or be angry with yourselves because you sold me," he told them. "God sent me before you to preserve life. God has made me lord of all Egypt. Go, bring our father here, and I will provide for all of you and your children." Moreover he kissed all his brothers and wept over them, and after that his brothers talked with him (Gen. 45:4–7, NKJV).

Did they beg forgiveness, try to explain why they had done it? All we know is they talked.

Webster defines *forgiveness* as "to absolve, to cease resentment, and to give up all claim." These action words require a decision.

Joseph forgave and was blessed to be with his father, Jacob, when he died. Joseph lived out his life in peace.

Can we say "Forgive them, Father"?

March 16

I love You, Lord, because You hear my voice and my prayer for mercy.

You bend down to listen.
I will pray as long as I have breath.
How kind You are!
How good You are!
You are merciful, O God, and so I walk in Your presence as I live here on earth. What can I offer You, Lord, for all You have done for me? I am Your servant, and I call upon Your name with thanksgiving.

I find joy in all You do for me because I know You love me and want the best for me.

You stepped into this world of darkness and brought light, revealing glory and majesty!

You are my God, and I will exalt You! (Ps. 116:1–2, 5, 9, 12, NLT)

> How sweet Your words taste to me;
> they are sweeter than honey.
>
> —Psalm 119:103, NLT

March 17

> Great and marvelous are Your works,
> O Lord God, the Almighty.
>
> —Revelation 15:3, NASB

Some people like birthdays; some not so much.

Sometimes when the calendar flips and it's my day, I'm neutral about it. Sometimes I'm passionate about it. But I am always fascinated about it—the gift of life from my Creator.

I read with wonder what the Bible tells me about Him. You saw me before I was born, and every day of my life was recorded in Your book. Every moment was laid out before a single day had passed (Ps. 139:16, NLT).

Our birthday—whether we ignore or celebrate our day of birth, it is recorded in heaven. We are not an accident nor are we a mistake. The Lord has made everything for His own purpose.

Whatever life has given us, or whatever it has denied us, one thing is certain: He has given us eternal life, and this life is in His Son. Whoever has the Son has life; whoever does not have God's Son does not have life (1 John 5:11–12, NLT).

March 18

Child, please don't worry about everyday life, whether you have enough food and drink, or enough clothes to wear.

Life is more than food and your body more than clothing. Look at the birds. They don't plant, harvest, or store food in barns. I feed them and care for them. You are far more valuable to Me than they are! Can all your worries add a single moment to your life?

Look at the lilies of the field and how they grow. They don't work or make their clothing, yet Solomon in all his glory was not dressed as beautifully as they are. And if I care so wonderfully for wildflowers that are here today and thrown into the fire tomorrow, I will certainly care for you. Why do you have so little faith?

So please don't worry about what you will eat or drink; what you will wear. I already know all your needs. It is foolish to worry about tomorrow, for tomorrow will bring its own worries. Today's trouble is enough for today (Matt. 6:26–34, NLT).

Seek Me above all else, live righteously, and I will give you everything you need.

March 19

I ask that You give me complete knowledge of Your will and spiritual wisdom and understanding. Then I will live with honor and always please You, Lord. My life will produce every kind of good fruit. All the while I will grow as I learn to know You better and better.

Strengthen me with all Your glorious power so I will have all the endurance and patience that I need. My confidence in You, O God, helps me discover confidence in myself as I face the challenges ahead.

Fill me with joy and thankfulness in every circumstance.

You have enabled me to share in the inheritance that belongs to Your people, who live in the light.

For You have rescued me from the kingdom of darkness and brought me safe into the kingdom of Your dear Son, who purchased my freedom and forgave my sins (Col. 1:9–13, NLT).

> How sweet Your words taste to me;
> they are sweeter than honey.
>
> —Psalm 119:103, NLT

March 20

> My problems go from bad to worse.
> Oh, save me from them all!
>
> —Psalm 25:17, NLT

The greatest burden we have to carry in life is self. The most difficult thing we have to manage is self. Our own daily living, our frames and feelings, our special weaknesses and temptations, our peculiar temperaments, our inward affairs of every kind—these are the things that perplex and worry us more than anything else and that bring us most often into bondage and darkness.

In laying off your burdens, therefore, the first one you must get rid of is yourself. You must hand yourself and all your inward experiences, your temptations, your temperament, your frames, and your feelings all over into the care and keeping of your God and leave them there. He made you, and therefore He understands you and knows how to manage you, and you must trust Him to do it.[6]

March 21

Paul tells the Philippians, "Every time I think of You, I give thanks to my God. And when I pray, I pray with joy for all of you, asking God's blessings on all you do, to shower you with joy and abiding trust" (Phil. 1:3, NLT).

Saul, later called Paul, was a Pharisee, one of the strictest sects of Judaism. He was religious and knew the Bible. But he believed that the Christian movement was a threat to Judaism. He persecuted and imprisoned followers of Jesus, both men and women.

When God called him into service, He transformed his life. It was sudden. He was on his way to Damascus to bring the Christians to Jerusalem in chains. While on the road approaching Damascus, a light from heaven flashed around him, and he fell to the ground. A voice said to him, "Saul, Saul, why are you persecuting Me?"

He said, "Who are You, Lord?" He answered, "I am Jesus whom you are persecuting; get up and enter the city, and it will be told you what you must do."

Paul personally met Jesus. His life would never be the same. And neither is ours when we meet Him.

> O love divine! Whose constant beam
> Shines on the eyes that will not see,
> And waits to bless us, while we dream
> Thou leavest us because we turn from Thee. (J. G.
>   Whittier)

March 22

Live for today!

> I'll never see this day again
> The seconds or the hours
> Now's the time to take the time
> To stop and smell the flowers
> Today's the day to give that smile
> And happiness away
> That you were saving for a friend

Some rainy, gloomy day.
This day is golden, priceless.
God made this day for you,
That deed you do for someone else,
May just come back to you.
So touch a heart, hold a hand,
Call that lonely friend,
Don't postpone the love you have.
This day won't come again. (Unknown)

March 23

My thoughts are all over the charts this morning racing from concern to fear. I can't seem to arrest them.

Why do I vacillate so much? One minute I trust You to handle what concerns me; the next minute I am baffled as what I can do to resolve my unrest.

Foolish me!

I know the only place I find peace is with You. That is heart knowledge. But head knowledge seems to have a mind of its own!

Ground me!

Penetrate my mind and my heart so that I have thoughts of love so deep for You there is room for nothing else.

All things are possible with You!

Hear me as I pray, O Lord. Be merciful and answer me!

I am confident in You, for the Lord is the Spirit, and wherever the Spirit of the Lord is, there is freedom (2 Cor. 3:17, NLT).

Yes, freedom from concern and fear! All praise to You!

> Hope has a thick skin and will endure many a blow; it will put on patience as a vestment and will endure all things (if they be of the right kind) for the joy that is set before it. Hence patience is called patience of hope,' because it is hope that makes the soul exercise long-suffering under the cross until the time comes to enjoy the crown!
>
> —John Bunyan

March 24

> And he was called the friend of God.
>
> —James 2:23, NASB

Abraham is called the friend of God. Why would God need or want a friend? He was complete in Himself. Yet in His sovereignty He chose Abraham. He made a covenant with him.

> I will make you into a great nation. I will bless you
> and make you famous, and you will be a blessing to
> others. I will bless those who bless you and curse
> those who treat you with contempt. All the fami-
> lies on earth will be blessed through you. (Gen.
> 12:2–3, NLT)

Abraham was a tower of faith. He obeyed God even to the point of his willingness to sacrifice his own son, Isaac. But he wasn't perfect.

Twice he passed off his wife, Sarah, as his sister to spare himself.

God chose imperfect men to fulfill His perfect plan. When we look at the lives of some of His chosen—among them Moses, Saul, David, and Jesus's handpicked disciples—we realize that God doesn't transform us and then call us. It is difficult to comprehend that a mighty God such as ours would take the infirmities of our personality and use them for His good.

We can take our hope in the life of one such as Abraham. When he lied about Sarah, he had lost faith in God's protection and provision. But his deception backfired, and God kept His covenant promise intact.

We are the imperfect children of a perfect God! And although our humanness gets in the way of His plan, He rescues us and brings us back into alignment with His will.

March 25

I can be judgmental. Why do I do that? For what gives me the right to make judgment calls about others when I know little or nothing about them or their circumstances?

Jesus's words strike a resounding call to us:

- Do not judge, and you will not be judged; and do not condemn, and you will not be condemned; pardon, and you will be pardoned. Give, and it will be given to you. They will pour into your lap a good measure—pressed down, shaken together, *and* running over. For by your standard of measure it will be measured to you in return. (Luke 6:37–38, NASB)
- For in the way you judge, you will be judged; and by your standard of measure, it will be measured to you. (Matt. 7:2, NASB)
- When the time comes for Your return, You will bring our darkest secrets to light and will reveal our private motives. Only then, O God, will You give us whatever praise is due. (1 Cor. 4:5, 7, NLT)

Live by every word that comes
from the mouth of the Lord.

—Deuteronomy 8:3, NLT

March 26

> I am leaving you with a gift—peace of mind and
> heart. And the peace I give is a gift the world
> cannot give. So don't be troubled or afraid.
>
> —John 14:27, NLT

The world talks a lot about inner peace. Therapy sessions, counselors, and countless books offer the means to inner peace. Manufactured or manipulated peace is very fragile. It can be destroyed instantly by failure, doubt, fear, difficulty, guilt, shame, regret, sorrow, and any challenge made to your position or possessions.

Child, My peace cannot be produced on any human level. It is not subject to fluctuations and uncertainties of life. It is spiritual peace: an attitude of the heart and mind when you know deep down that all is well between you and Me and that I am lovingly in control of everything.

If you trust in Me, I promise to *keep* you in *perfect* peace. That means that you do not have to continually seek inner peace. It abides in you because your thoughts are fixed on Me. It is My gift to you.

The world can't give you this peace that I promise. Because of it, you will have no need to fear, neither will your heart to be troubled. For you can rest in the assurance that My peace goes beyond all you can imagine or ask for.

Open the gift! It is free!

March 27

> Lord, I am ready to go with You,
> both to prison and to death.
>
> —Luke 22:33, NKJV

It has been written that Peter was crucified. At his own request he was crucified with his head downward. Tradition has it that his brother, Andrew, was fastened to the cross not with nails, but with cords to make his death more lingering. He hung there two days praising God. The brothers made the ultimate sacrifice. It is believed that John was the only one of Jesus's original disciples who was not killed for his faith.

We haven't faced death in defense of our faith, but Jesus says there is a cost to follow Him. He laid it out clearly when He said if we want to follow Him, we have to take up our cross. We can kill those attitudes and sins that separate us from Him. We can nail them to the cross, cutting off the supply of nourishment that they need to survive. Replace pride with humility, greed with generosity; die to the world of materialism.

Jesus gives some startling measures we must take when He says to cut off our hand, foot, eye—whatever feeds our sinful nature. He uses these illustrations to stress the importance of ridding ourselves of the sin in our lives. It can mean giving up a relationship, habit, or even a job that is nurturing sin. For some, that can be as painful as cutting off a limb or losing an eye. But nothing should stand in the way of following Him. Jesus says we must be determined to remove the sin in our lives or face the unquenchable fire of hell.

Are we ready to do that?

> Commit yourself wholeheartedly
> to these words of Mine.
>
> —Deuteronomy 11:18

March 28

> See to it that no one takes you captive through philosophy and empty deception, according to the tradition of men, according to the elementary principles of the world, rather than according to Christ. For in Him all the fullness of Deity dwells in bodily form, and in Him you have been made complete, and He is the head over all rule and authority.
>
> —Colossians 2:8–10, NASB

Child, let your roots grow down into Me, and let your life be built on Me. Then your faith will grow strong in the truth you were taught, and you will overflow with thankfulness.

Don't let anyone capture you with empty philosophies and high-sounding nonsense that come from human thinking and from the spiritual powers of this world rather than from Me. All the fullness of God lives in Me.

So you also are complete through your union with Me, for I am the head over every ruler and authority.

Blessed are those who trust in Me and have made Me their hope and confidence. They are like trees planted along a riverbank, with roots that reach deep into the water. Such trees are not bothered by the heat or worried by long months of drought. Their leaves stay green, and they never stop producing fruit (Jer. 17:7–8, NLT).

> Your Word is a lamp for my feet,
> a light on my path.
>
> —Psalm 119:105, NLT

March 29

> Now godliness with contentment is great gain.
>
> —1 Timothy 6:6, NKJV

We may not have control over the circumstances, but we have control over how we deal with them. Worry wearies us. It robs us of health, peace, and joy. It drains us of the ability to function as we should. We must keep our eyes focused on Him, trusting in His provision.

Lord, I want to be content with whatever I have. You will never fail me nor abandon me, generously providing all I need. Help me surrender any desire for possessions that I do not need.

Free me from concern about tomorrow: what I will eat and what I will wear. I brought nothing with me when I came into this world, and I can take nothing with me when I leave it. So if I have enough food and clothing, I will be content.

> He is rich who is content with the least; for
> contentment is the wealth of nature.
>
> —Socrates

March 30

In *The Book of Forgiving*, Desmond and Mpho Tutu write:

> The invitation to forgive is not an invitation to for-
> get. Nor is it an invitation to claim that an injury

is less hurtful than it really was. Nor is it a request to paper over the fissure in a relationship, to say it's okay when it's not.

It's not okay to be injured. It's not okay to be abused. It's not okay to be violated. It's not okay to be betrayed. But it is okay to forgive.

Forgiveness opens the door to peace between people, and opens the space for peace within each person. The victim cannot have peace without forgiving. The perpetrator will not have genuine peace while unforgiven. There cannot be peace between victim and perpetrator while the injury lies between them.

The invitation to forgive is an invitation to search out the perpetrator's humanity. When we forgive, we recognize the reality that there, but for the grace of God, go I. The invitation to forgive is an invitation to find healing and peace.

Forgiveness is a choice, but it's not an option.

—Joel Osteen

March 31

> And behold, the veil of the temple was torn in
> two from top to bottom; and the earth shook and
> the rocks were split. The tombs were opened, and
> many bodies of the saints who had fallen asleep
> were raised; and coming out of the tombs after
> His resurrection they entered the holy city and
> appeared to many.
>
> —Matthew 27:51–53, NASB

When His beloved Son died on the cross, God responded with colossal gestures in nature. He blanketed the land in darkness, tore the temple veil in two, raised the dead, and shook the earth. The agony was over; Jesus's work was finished. The Father responded.

It is fitting that creation should have trembled; mankind, whom God had created, crucified Him. Seven hundred years before Christ was born, Isaiah had written about what would happen that day.

Crucifixion hadn't even been heard of then. It would later become a Roman form of execution. It was a slow and painful death.

Christ died for us that we might be reconciled to God. He was a man of sorrows—scourged, afflicted, pierced, and crushed.

Father, all the earth felt Your response at the death of Your beloved Son. I cannot comprehend the suffering He endured to redeem me. I am grateful for His sacrifice that has brought me reconciliation with You, my Creator.

April 1

> I have called you by name; you are Mine.
>
> —Isaiah 43:1, NASB

Child, don't be afraid. I have redeemed you. I call you by your name, for you are Mine. Do you know that I created you for My glory? Do you know that because I abide in you, nothing or no one can harm you? You are secure in Me. You are precious to Me, and I love you.

I am your Light and your Salvation; there is nothing or no one you should fear. I am the defense of your life.

Trust only in Me. I have taken you into My embrace, shielding you from harm and tenderly leading you along the right path.

I know you and call you by name. Nothing can separate you from My love.

If troubles spring up in an unexpected way today, take hold of My promise that you will not drown; you will not be burned.

> How sweet Your words taste to me;
> they are sweeter than honey.

—Psalm 119:103, NLT

April 2

God showed how much He loved us by sending His one and only Son into the world so that we might have eternal life through Him. This is real love—not that we loved God, but that He loved us, and sent His Son as a sacrifice to take away our sins.

Dear friends, since God loved us that much, we surely ought to love each other. No one has ever seen God. But if we love each other, God lives in us, and His love is brought to full expression in us.

And God has given us His Spirit as proof that we live in Him and He in us. Furthermore, we have seen with our own eyes and now testify that the Father sent His Son to be the Savior of the world. All who declare that Jesus is the Son of God have God living in them, and they live in God. God loves us, and we have put our trust in His love.

God is love, and all who live in love live in God, and God lives in them (1 John 4:16, NLT).

The very essence of Your words is truth.

—Psalm 119:160, NLT

April 3

Who will protect me from the wicked?
Who will stand up for me against evildoers?

—Psalm 94:16, NLT

Thoughts that disturb and trouble us seldom come from God. It is generally best to put them away, and throw yourself with increased trust in Him and mistrust of self, at His feet.

And never forget amid whatever may befall you—dryness, coldness, desolation, and disappointment, consciousness of many faults, and of great weakness, and want of faith—that where love is, there God is sure to be. He never yet has suffered any soul to fall wholly from Him who amid all its frailties and falls, clings to Him in love.[7]

When doubts disturb my troubled breast,
And all is dark as night to me,
Here, as on solid rock, I rest,
That so it seemeth good to Thee. (Ray Palmer)

April 4

O God, You are my God; I earnestly search for You.
My soul thirsts for You; my whole body longs for
    You in this parched and weary land.
I gaze upon Your power and glory.
Your unfailing love is better than life itself; how I
    praise You!
I will praise You as long as I live, lifting up my hands
    to You in prayer.
I will praise You with songs of joy.
I lie awake thinking of You, meditating on You
    through the night.
You are my Helper, my Confidant.
I sing for joy in the shadow of Your wings.
I cling to You; Your strong right hand holds me
    securely.
I cherish Your tender love for me. (Ps. 63:1–8, NLT)

April 5

What a compassionate God we serve! He is the source of
mercy and the One who comforts and strengthens us in
hardship and trial.

We read of the woman who had hemorrhaged for twelve years. She had spent all she had on doctors, but had grown worse.

Hearing that Jesus was near, she joined the crowd, and pushed her way through, moving closer to Him. She was terribly frightened because she knew that her constant bleeding made her ritually unclean, and if she touched Jesus, it would cause Him to be unclean under Jewish law. What would He do if He discovered what she had done?

It would be a bold move. But she continued to shove closer. She thought, *If I just touch His garments, I will get well.* She came up behind Him and touched His cloak.

Instantly the flow of her blood stopped! Jesus, aware of the power going out from Him, turned around in the crowd and said, "Who touched My garments?"

His disciples said, "Look at the size of this crowd pressing all around You and you ask, 'Who touched Me?'"

He looked around and saw the woman. She was trembling. He motioned for her to come closer. The crowd watched as she moved toward Jesus. She fell down before Him and told Him it was her. Then she told Him of the miracle.

He said to her, "Daughter, your faith has made you well; go in peace and be healed of your affliction" (Mark 5:34, NASB).

We must never hold back from reaching out in faith to Jesus. The woman didn't let her fear keep her from God. We don't need to face the difficult trials alone. Reach out in faith and expectation and touch His garment.

April 6

Psalm 119 is the longest psalm and the longest chapter in the Bible—176 verses. I avoided it when I first began to read the Bible. It was too full of decrees, instructions, and commands. I assumed it was for those who lived in Old Testament days, and I didn't think it had that much to do with me. I wasn't studying the Bible to become a scholar or to learn about decrees and such. I was seeking God.

As we mature spiritually, we become acutely aware that God isn't going to automatically zap us with the knowledge of His Word. We have to apply ourselves with diligence and discipline in order to learn about Him. It is a gradual process of growing from infancy to adulthood.

We can never know all God has for us to learn, but Psalm 119 gives us guidance.

God's Word reveals His love for us. His commandments are for our good. And so we pray:

> Teach me Your decrees, O Lord; I will keep them
> to the end.

Give me understanding and I will obey Your instructions; I will put them into practice with all my heart.

Make me walk along the path of Your commands, for that is where my happiness is found.

Give me an eagerness for Your laws rather than a love for money!

Turn my eyes from worthless things, and give me life through Your Word.

Reassure me of Your promise, made to those who fear You.

Help me abandon my shameful ways; for Your regulations are good.

I long to obey Your commandments! Renew my life with Your goodness. (Ps. 119:33–40, NLT)

April 7

Coming out, He went to the Mount of Olives, as He was accustomed, and His disciples also followed Him. When He came to the place, He said to them, "Pray that you may not enter into temptation."

And He was withdrawn from them about a stone's throw, and He knelt down and prayed, saying, "Father, if it is Your will, take this cup away from Me; nevertheless not My will, but Yours, be done."

Then an angel appeared to Him from heaven, strengthening Him.

And being in agony, He prayed more earnestly.

Then His sweat became like great drops of blood falling down to the ground. (Luke 22:39–44, NKJV)

People do not live by bread alone, but by every word that comes from the mouth of God.

—Matthew 4:4, NLT

April 8

Jesus, You are the head of the church, which is Your body. You are the beginning, supreme over all who rise from the dead.

You are first in everything, for God the Father in all His fullness was pleased to live in You. Through You, He reconciled everything to Himself.

He made peace with everything in heaven and on earth by means of Your blood on the cross. This includes all of us who were once far away from God. We were Your enemies, separated from You by our evil thoughts and actions.

Yet now You have reconciled us to Yourself through Your death in Your physical body. As a result, You have brought us into Your own presence, and we are holy and blameless as we stand before You without a single fault (Col. 1:18–22, NLT).

Such knowledge is too wonderful for me to comprehend!

> The grass withers and the flowers fade, but the
> Word of our God stands forever.

—Isaiah 40:8, NLT

April 9

I honor You Lord for Your glory and strength.

I honor You for the glory of Your name.

I worship You Lord in the splendor of Your holiness.

Your voice echoes above the sea.

Your glory thunders over the mighty sea.

Your voice is powerful and majestic. It splits the mighty cedars; shatters the cedars of Lebanon. You make Lebanon's mountains skip like a calf. You make Mount Hermon leap like a young wild ox.

Your voice strikes with bolts of lightning, and makes the barren wilderness quake; You shake the wilderness of Kadesh.

Your voice twists mighty oaks and strips the forests bare.

In Your temple everyone shouts, "Glory!"

You rule over the floodwaters. You reign as King forever.

You give me strength and bless me with peace.

I will praise Your name forever! (Ps. 29:2–11, NLT)

April 10

Child, I am Your Father. You are the clay, I am the Potter. You are formed by My hand.

When you call on Me, I will answer, I will be with you in trouble. I will rescue and honor you, and I will reward you with a long life and give you My salvation (Ps. 91:15–16, NLT).

You are My masterpiece. I created you anew in Jesus so that I can do the things I planned for you long ago

I hold the depths of the earth and the mightiest mountains in My hands. I hold you in the palm of My hand; the hand that formed you.

Such knowledge is too wonderful to me, my Lord and Creator. All honor and glory be to You, O Most High God.

Oh, what blessed communion when in the Potter's hands, we will be shaped into a vessel of honor fit for the Master's use.

April 11

> He said, "It is finished!" And He bowed
> His head and gave up His spirit.
>
> —John 19:30, NASB

Crucifixion was intentionally slow, meant to inflict as much pain and suffering as possible before dying.

Christ took all sin upon Himself so that those who believe in Him might escape the penalty from sin. He was the ultimate sacrifice, and God's work of salvation was finished.

We grieve when we read of His horrendous suffering and death, knowing what He endured for us, that we might be made right with God.

We can make David's cry of forgiveness ours.

> Be gracious to me, O God, according to Your lovingkindness; according to the greatness of Your compassion blot out my transgressions.
>
> Wash me thoroughly from my iniquity and cleanse me from my sin.
>
> For I know my transgressions, and my sin is ever before me.
>
> Against You, You only, I have sinned and done what is evil in Your sight,

so that You are justified when You speak and blameless when You judge.

Purify me, I shall be clean; wash me, I shall be whiter than snow. (Ps. 51:1–4, NASB)

Create in me a clean heart, O God and renew a steadfast spirit within me.

Do not cast me away from Your presence and do not take Your Holy Spirit from me.

Restore to me the joy of Your salvation and sustain me with a willing spirit. (Ps. 51:11–12, NASB)

April 12

I long to enjoy life and see many happy days.

To keep my tongue from speaking evil, and my lips from telling lies.

To turn from evil and do good.

To search for peace and work to maintain it.

I know Your eyes watch over me as I strive to do right.

And I know Your ears are open to my prayers.

Do not turn Your face from me. (1 Pet. 3:10–12, NLT)

Fill me with Your Spirit and shower me with grace so that I can strive to achieve all that You would have for me to do.

These instructions will lead to a life free from those human faults and failings that take me away from You.

I am not surprised by my sinfulness. But I am amazed by Your forgiveness and grace.

April 13

> But go, tell His disciples—and Peter—that He is going before you into Galilee; there you will see Him, as He said to you.
>
> —Mark 16:7, NKJV

The Son of God rose from the dead, and no one witnessed it. The evidence was there—an empty tomb, discarded linen wrappings. The most powerfully divine event in history took place in a secluded garden.

Angels quietly announced the news. Those who believed He had risen experienced Him. To one, He simply said her name: "Mary!" That day He walked beside two of them, and in the evening they dined.

When we accept Christ as our Savior, it takes place in the seclusion of our hearts. The evidence is there. We are made new; our old ways discarded. The Good News is proclaimed in heaven by hosts of angels. And we experience Him. He calls us by name, walks with us, and dines with us. And one day, we too will be resurrected by the same divine power that raised Jesus from the dead.

It is a glorious Easter morning sunrise at the beach. I am awed by the fathomless power behind an ocean larger than the total land area of the world. God's almighty power that is at work in the universe is working in us. To Him be the power and the glory. Alleluia!

Jesus, I accept You as my Lord and Savior. Alleluia!

April 14

> O Lord, You are my Light and my Salvation,
>   so why should I be afraid?
>
> —Psalm 27:1, NASB

You are my Fortress, protecting me from danger, so why should I tremble?

The one thing I ask of You, Lord—the thing I seek most—is to live in Your house all the days of my life, delighting in Your perfections and meditating in Your temple (Ps. 27:4, NASB).

Hear me as I pray, O Lord. Be merciful and answer me! My heart has heard You say, "Come and talk with me."

And my heart responds, "Lord, I am coming." Do not turn Your back on me. Do not reject Your servant.

You have always been my Helper. Don't abandon me now, O God of my salvation! Even if my father and mother abandon me, You will hold me close.

Teach me how to live, O Lord. Lead me along the right path.

I am confident that I will see Your goodness and I wait patiently for You.

I will be brave and courageous as I wait for You (Ps. 27:7–11, NASB).

> Your Word is a lamp for my feet,
> a light on my path.
>
> —Psalm 119:105, NLT

April 15

> I wait quietly before God, for my
> victory comes from Him.
>
> —Psalm 62:1, NLT

I feel You in the good moments when things are on cruise control, and I can relax in Your love.

But I am humbly grateful to feel You in the dark moments—when circumstances are out of my control, and I feel as though I am heading for a cliff.

That is when You lift me up! High above the natural to a supernatural where I cling to You, feel Your peace and bask in Your love.

Thank You for each day You carry me in Your arms. I wait quietly before You, for my victory comes from You.

You alone are my Rock and my Salvation—my Fortress where I will never be shaken.

> Each wish to pray is a breath from heaven, to
> strengthen and refresh us; each act of faith, done
> to amend our prayers, is wrought in us by Him,
> and draws us to Him, and His gracious look on us.
> Neglect nothing which can produce reverence.
>
> —Edward B. Pusey

April 16

Jesus asks, Would anyone light a lamp and then put it under a basket or under a bed? Of course not! A lamp is placed on a stand, where its light will shine.

For everything that is hidden will eventually be brought into the open, and every secret will be brought to light.

Anyone with ears to hear should listen and understand.

Pay close attention to what you hear, My child. The closer you listen, the more understanding you will be given, and you will receive even more.

To those who listen to My teaching, more understanding will be given. But for those who are not listening, even what little understanding they have will be taken away from them (Mark 4:21–25, NLT).

If a lamp isn't used to help people see, it is useless. And if we have a lamp why would we hide it under a basket? Maybe we don't know we are hiding it. Maybe it is hidden under complacency or resistance to obey. Whatever the basket might be, we need to get rid of it.

He lives in us. All those with whom we come in contact with will see His radiant light within.

Because of that, we can be a light to others who cannot see Him.

In the same way, let your light shine before others, that they may see your good deeds and glorify your Father in heaven.

> People do not live by bread alone, but by every
> word that comes from the mouth of God.
>
> —Matthew 4:4, NLT

April 17

The Our Father is a prayer that most of us learned in childhood.

> Our Father Who is in heaven,
> Hallowed be Your name.
> Your kingdom come.
> Your will be done,
> On earth as it is in heaven.
> Give us this day our daily bread.
> And forgive us our debts, as we also have forgiven our debtors.
> And do not lead us into temptation, but deliver us from evil.
> For Yours is the kingdom and the power and the glory forever. (Matt. 6:9–13, NASB)

Maybe we have said it so much in our lifetime that we don't grasp the depth of this conversation with God. There is not one instance of *me*, *I*, or *my*. We address the Father with *us*, *we*, and *our*.

Larry and I say the Our Father each night before turning out the lights. Our voices unite in talking with Our Father; a perfect way to end a day.

Prayer is the nearest approach to God and the
highest enjoyment of Him that we are capable of
in this life.

—William Law

April 18

Give thanks to the Lord, for He is good!
His faithful love endures forever.

—Psalm 118:1, NLT

I give thanks to You O Lord, for You are good!

Your faithful love endures forever. In my distress I prayed
to You and You answered me and set me free.

I know that You are for me so I will have no fear.

What can mere people do to me? You help me, for it
is better to take refuge in You than to trust in people. (Ps.
118:5–7, NLT)

You are my strength and my song (Ps. 118:14, NLT).

I thank You for answering my prayer and giving me victory! (Ps. 118:21, NLT)

This is the day that You have made and I will rejoice and
be glad in it. (Ps. 118:24, NLT)

You are my God, and I will praise You!

I give You thanks for You are good!

Your faithful love endures forever. (Ps. 118:28–29, NLT)

How sweet Your words taste to me;
they are sweeter than honey.

—Psalm 119:103, NLT

April 19

Child, who will want to harm you if you are eager to do good? But even if you suffer for doing what is right, I will reward you for it. So don't worry or be afraid of their threats.

Instead, you must worship Me as Lord of your life. And if someone asks about your hope as a believer, always be ready to explain it. But do this in a gentle and respectful way.

Keep your conscience clear. Then if people speak against you, they will be ashamed when they see what a good life you live because you belong to Me.

Remember, it is better to suffer for doing good—if that is what I want—than to suffer for doing wrong!

I suffered for your sins once for all time. I never sinned, but I died for you to bring you safely home to the Father. I suffered physical death, but I was raised to life in the Spirit (1 Pet. 3:13–18, NLT).

Commit yourself wholeheartedly
to these words of Mine.

—Deuteronomy 11:18, NLT

April 20

Jesus desires to be even closer to us than a brother or a friend. He is not only the God who is above us and the God who has come among us; He is also the God who desires to dwell within us. This is the fact that the apostle Paul described in Colossians 1:27 as "the glorious riches of this mystery, which is Christ in you, the hope of glory." It is the wonder he describes in Galatians 2:20 when he says, "I have been crucified with Christ and I no longer live, but Christ lives in me."

This is the mystery we were made to contain: the very life of Jesus. He means to live out the reality of who He is right here within the reality of who we are. He means to be our lives—the breath of our lungs, the thoughts in our heads, the energy and creativity in our jobs, the love in our hearts. He means to take on the stress and unravel the inner complications so that we can move through our lives just as He did, in gentleness and simplicity and harmony.

We were never intended to be more than containers: temples to contain His glory (1 Cor. 3:16–17), branches to contain the sap of his life (John 15:1–8), vessels to contain the new wine of His Spirit (Rom. 9:20–21). We are the glove, He is the hand. We are the cup, He is the coffee. We are the lamp, He is the light.

This is what we were made for. This is the intended purpose of the human person and personality—not to be gods, but to be filled with God. This is the kind of unity that was present in the garden but is sadly missing in our world today. It is the sheer simplicity of God's design that was shattered by humanity's sin. And it is the reason Jesus came and cared and was tortured, killed, laid in a tomb, and raised to life again—so that He could give us another shot at being what we were intended to be: united with God in oneness, in Spirit and Truth.[8]

April 21

I sit here in my prayer corner this morning and read Your Word. Some of Your instructions seem beyond my human capacity to follow. They are! Only by Your power can I strive to obey Your commands.

Here I read:

> All of you should be of one mind. Sympathize with each other.
>
> Love each other as brothers and sisters.

Be tenderhearted, and keep a humble attitude.

Don't repay evil for evil.

Don't retaliate with insults when people insult you. Instead, pay them back with a blessing.

That is what God has called you to do, and He will grant you His blessing.

If you want to enjoy life and see many happy days, keep your tongue from speaking evil and your lips from telling lies.

Turn away from evil and do good.

Search for peace, and work to maintain it.

The eyes of the Lord watch over those who do right, and His ears are open to their prayers. But the Lord turns His face against those who do evil. (1 Pet. 3:8–12, NLT)

> Live by every word that comes
> from the mouth of the Lord.
>
> —Deuteronomy 8:3, NLT

April 22

> Blessed *are* the pure in heart,
> for they shall see God.
>
> —Matthew 5:8, NKJV

Pure! *Webster* says it means not mixed with anything else; clean and not harmful in any way.

I want a pure heart. To me that means nothing else is mixed with my love of God. It is pure, as gold is pure, making it precious in the sight of the Lord. When I mix my heart with the values that the world sees as good, then my heart is contaminated—tainted!

When I examine my life, I realize it starts with my thoughts. "For as he thinks within himself, so he is" (Prov. 23:7, NASB).

"The good man out of the good treasure of his heart brings forth what is good; and the evil man out of the evil treasure brings forth what is evil; for his mouth speaks from that which fills his heart" (Luke 6:45, NASB).

"Out of the heart proceed evil thoughts, murders, adulteries, fornications, thefts, false witness, blasphemies. These are the things which defile a man" (Matt. 15:19, NASB).

"The Lord does not see as man sees; for man looks at the outward appearance, but the Lord looks at the heart" (1 Sam. 16:7, NASB).

O Lord, I want to keep my way pure by keeping it according to Your Word. With all my heart I have sought You; do not let me wander from Your commandments. Your Word I have treasured in my heart, that I may not sin against You.

Create in me a pure heart, O Lord, that You may be glorified in all I think, say and do. And renew me with a steadfast spirit.

April 23

Ponderings on prayer:

It is said that God's phone number is Jeremiah 33:3.

Call to Me and I will answer you, and I will tell you great and mighty things, which you do not know. (Jer. 33:3, NASB)

The LORD hears his people when they *call* to Him for help. He rescues them from all their troubles. (Ps. 34:17, NLT)

Don't worry about anything; instead, pray about everything. *Tell* God what you need, and thank Him for all He has done. (Phil. 4:6, NLT)

I also tell you this: If two of you agree here on earth concerning anything you *ask*, My Father in heaven will do it for you. (Matt. 18:19, NLT)

Keep on *asking*, and you will receive what you *ask* for. Keep on seeking, and you will find. Keep on knocking, and the door will be opened to you. (Matt. 7:7, NLT)

Call Him!

> Now all glory to God, who is able, through His
> mighty power at work within us, to accomplish
> infinitely more than we might ask or think.
>
> —Ephesians 3:20, NLT

April 24

> And we have a priceless inheritance—an
> inheritance that is kept in heaven for you, pure and
> undefiled, beyond the reach of change and decay.
>
> —1 Peter 1:4, NLT

Inheritance is the practice of passing on property, titles, debts, rights, and obligations upon the death of an individual.

In the theological sense, to inherit means to receive an irrevocable gift, with an emphasis on the special relationship between the benefactor and the recipients. Unlike legal inheritance, the benefactor, God, does not die, yet He provides material and spiritual blessings because we are His children.

Child, you can live with great expectation because you have this inestimable inheritance.

Your mind cannot comprehend its value. And through your faith, I am protecting you by My power until you receive this salvation which is ready to be revealed on the last day for all to see. There is a wonderful joy ahead for you, even though you must endure many trials for a little while. These trials will show that your faith is genuine.

It is being tested as fire tests and purifies gold; though your faith is far more precious to Me than mere gold. When your faith remains strong through many trials, it will bring you much praise and glory and honor on the day when I am revealed to the whole world (1 Pet. 1:3–7, NLT).

And on that day, you will be with Me, enjoying the priceless inheritance I have promised.

Pain or pleasure? It makes no difference to me, Lord, for I know You will provide all I need for I am Your child. I look forward to the day when I am with You. All praise to You, Father of my Lord, Jesus.

April 25

> My grace is all you need. My power works best
> in weakness. So now I am glad to boast about my
> weaknesses, so that the power of Christ can work
> through me.
>
> —2 Corinthians 12:9, NLT

Child, look away from the imperfections you find in yourself. Turn to Me and behold My loveliness, My perfection.

The time you spend centered on rebuking yourself robs us of the sweet communion I desire.

There will be moments in this day that may drag you down when discouraged with your mistakes. There might be times when you think, *Why did I do that? Why did I say that?*

You are impatient and recognize that the person you want to be isn't always the person you are.

Don't allow that to dictate your life! Reach for Me to find calm. The more you practice this, you will be enabled to find your perfection in Me. My grace is all you need. My power works best in weakness.

Align yourself with My power and wisdom.

Oh Lord, my health may fail, and my spirit may grow weak, but You remain the strength of my heart. You are mine forever and will generously provide all I need with plenty left over to share with others (2 Cor. 9:8, NLT).

I need not depend on myself for perfection. I will be renewed this day by Your blessed perfection that works through me.

April 26

> If someone says, "I love God," and hates his
> brother, he is a liar; for the one who does not love
> his brother whom he has seen, cannot love God
> whom he has not seen.
>
> —1 John 4:20, NLT

Our love for God will be measured by our everyday treatment of those we encounter. It is easy to *say* we love Him when it doesn't cost us anything. But the proof lies deep in our hearts, the very essence of who we are. It will manifest itself without struggle or thought. Love is not evident just in our actions but in our thoughts and feelings.

And that is where it begins. God is the source of all human love. We love because He first loved us. When we love God, the Holy Spirit kindles such a fire in us that it overflows to those around us.

We can't fool ourselves by saying, "I just love everyone!" We don't. We all have different ideas about love. Love of spouse, family, and friends come easier for some of us. Loving the unkind, bitter, spiteful person is a challenge.

We can never love as God loves. For He *is* Love. *Agape* love is the Greek word for the most self-sacrificing love that there is: the type of love God has for us, His children. It was the love He displayed on the cross.

Lord, I will never attain that kind of love. But I pray that because of Your love for me, I can love the unloved. Today I will look beyond my circle of loved ones, for those who don't know love, and show them a glimpse of You.

April 27

I randomly open my Bible this morning, allowing You to direct me to the verses You would have me read.

Psalm 71:5 reminds me to live with trust; trust that knows no boundaries.

Proverbs 16:1 reminds me that I can make my plans, but You, O Lord, have the right answers.

Psalm 119:105 reminds me that Your Word is a lamp unto my feet.

Titus 3:7 tells me that because of Your grace, You declared me righteous and assure me of eternal life.

1 Corinthians 2:9 declares that no eye has seen, no ear has heard, and no mind has imagined what You have prepared for those of us who love You.

At times I have such a longing to be in Your Word that I can physically feel it. I am left with no choice but to drop what I am doing and come here to be with You. I have found what I was looking for!

I love You!

April 28

Then James and John, asked Jesus for a favor.
"What is your request?" He asked.

They replied, "When You sit on Your glorious throne, we want to sit in places of honor next to You, one on Your right and the other on Your left."

Jesus said, "You don't know what you are asking! Are you able to drink from the bitter cup of suffering I am about to drink? Are you able to be baptized with the baptism of suffering I must be baptized with?"

"Oh yes," they replied. "We are able!"

Then Jesus told them, "You will indeed drink from My bitter cup and be baptized with My baptism of suffering. But I have no right to say who will sit on My right or My left. God has prepared those places for the ones He has chosen."

When the ten other disciples heard what James and John had asked, they were indignant. So Jesus called them together and said, "You know that the rulers in this world lord it over their people, and officials flaunt their authority over those under them. But among you it will be different.

Whoever wants to be a leader among you must be your servant, and whoever wants to be first among you must be the slave of everyone else. For even the Son of Man came not to be served but to serve others and to give His life as a ransom for many." (Mark 10:35–45, NLT)

Does not My Word burn like fire? says the Lord.
Is it not like a mighty hammer that smashes a rock
to pieces?

—Jeremiah 23:29, NLT

April 29

So do not worry about tomorrow; for tomorrow
will care for itself. Each day has enough trouble of
its own.

—Matthew 6:34, NASB

Lord, You tell me not to worry about tomorrow, for tomorrow will bring its own worries. I am reminded that I have access only to this moment. Everything else is unpredictable. I want to live in the present.

You tell me to keep on doing what is right and trust my life to the You who created me, for You will never fail me.

I am awed when I realize You are in charge of every breath I take. I put my hand to my mouth and breathe into it. I feel the warm breath against my palm. I breathe in deeply and release it. I hear it!

O yes, My Lord and my God, I trust my life to You

> Sorrow looks back, Worry looks around,
> Faith looks up.
>
> —Ralph Waldo Emerson

April 30

I can't begin to understand the incredible greatness of God's power for me. This is the same mighty power that raised Jesus from the dead and seated Him in the place of honor at the Father's right hand in the heavenly realms.

Now He is far above any ruler or authority or power or leader or anything else—not only in this world, but also in the world to come. All things have been put under His authority and have made Him head over all things for the benefit of the church. And the church is His body; it is made full and complete by Jesus, who fills all things everywhere with Himself (Eph. 1:19–23, NASB).

Lord, I ask for Your spiritual wisdom and insight so that I might grow in my knowledge of You. I pray that my heart will be flooded with light so that I can understand the confident hope You have given me.

May 1

> I will refresh the weary and satisfy the faint.
>
> —Jeremiah 31:25, NIV

I'm sitting in the waiting room for an early-morning doctor appointment. A young woman rushes in, and slips into her desk behind the check-in counter. Her coworker asks, "How are you today?"

"I'm tired," she sighs.

I feel bad for her and ask God to help her through her day.

"I'm tired," is a mantra for many. Why wouldn't we be tired? Slumping along under the weight of unpaid bills, rebellious children, stuck in a job that's going nowhere, unresolved health issues—the list goes on. Sleepless nights offer no answers, no peace.

I think of Jesus and the times He must have been sleep-deprived and exhausted. The demands on Him came from every direction. Crowds followed Him everywhere.

The Bible tells us that Jesus prayed often—sometimes before daybreak, but always a place alone with His Father.

No matter how weary or stressed we are, we *can* pray. We may not be able to find the secluded place we long for, but we can pray.

We can keep it simple with an arrow prayer. "Lord, I am tired! Please help me through this day." It takes discipline, but it shows results. Prayer changes things. Prayer changes us!

Jesus promises He will refresh and satisfy us. We can face each day with Him through prayer. Why wouldn't we try it?

The cartoon character Dennis the Menace asked his neighbor Mr. Wilson, "When you can't sleep, do you count sheep?" Mr. Wilson replied, "No, I talk to the Shepherd."

> Truly my soul finds rest in God;
> my salvation comes from Him.
>
> —Psalm 62:1, NIV

May 2

I want to lead a life worthy of You for You have called me.

You instruct me to always be humble and gentle.

You tell me to be patient with others, making allowance for each other's faults because of my love.

I will make every effort to keep myself united in the Spirit. It will help bind me together with others in peace. For there is one body and one Spirit, just as I have been called to one glorious hope for the future.

My life is firmly rooted in You, O God. Therefore, I am empowered by You to be flexible with others—their ideas and points of view.

I won't be tossed and blown about by every wind of new teaching. Then I will no longer be immature like a child.

Thank You that because of Christ and my faith in You, I can now come boldly and confidently into Your presence.

May 3

> I've dreamed many dreams that never came true.
> I've seen them vanish at dawn,
> but I've realized enough of my dreams thank God,
>   to make me want to dream on.
> I've prayed many prayers when no answer came,
>   though I waited patient and long, but answers
>   have come to enough of my prayers to make me
>   keep praying on
> I've trusted many a friend who failed and left me to
>   weep alone, but I've found enough of my friends
>   true blue to make me keep trusting on
> I've sown many seeds that fell by the way for the
>   birds to feed upon,
> but I've held enough golden sheaves in my hand to
>   make me keep sowing on.

> I've drained the cup of disappointment and pain and gone many days without song, but I've supped enough nectar from the roses of life to make me want to live on. (Unknown)

May 4

Jesus, You are the visible image of the invisible God.

You existed before anything was created and are supreme over all creation.

For through You, God created everything in the heavenly realms and on earth.

You made things that I can see and the things I can't see, such as thrones, kingdoms, rulers, and authorities in the unseen world.

Everything was created through You and for You.

You existed before anything else, and hold all creation together (Col. 1:15–17, NLT).

For ever since the world was created, people have seen the earth and sky. Through everything God made, they can clearly see His invisible qualities—His eternal power and divine nature. So we have no excuse for not knowing God (Rom. 1:20, NLT).

By His Spirit, through His Word, for His glory!

May 5

> And David was dancing before the
> Lord with all *his* might.
>
> —2 Samuel 6:14, NASB

David brought the ark to Jerusalem, and he was so over-joyed he was dancing in the street.

There are times at Sunday services that my heart is over-joyed with God's love, the pleasure of worshiping with oth-ers, the preaching of His Word, the church filled with song, that I want to stand, throw my hands in the air, and shout, "Alleluia, Jesus!"

The reason for not giving into emotional display is influ-enced by the way I have worshiped from my earliest church attendance. It is more of a refrained reverence.

Matthew 6:1 says, "Beware of practicing your right-eousness before men to be noticed by them." Although my reason for outward expression of worship is not the need to be noticed, but it would be impossible not to draw atten-tion if I am the only one standing, raising my hands, and praising Jesus.

Matthew 6:6 says, "But you, when you pray, go into your inner room, close your door and pray to your Father who is in secret, and your Father who sees *what is done* in secret will reward you."

It is in the deepest recesses of our being, in the secret place of our heart, we can stand, throw up our hands, and shout, "Alleluia, Jesus" at Sunday services. He will hear us.

May 6

> Submit to God, and you will have peace;
> then things will go well for you.
>
> —Job 22:21, NLT

Let me not seek out of Thee what I can only find in Thee,
peace and rest and joy and bliss, which abide only in Thy abiding joy.
Lift up my soul above the weary round of harassing thoughts to Thy eternal presence.
Lift up my soul to the pure, bright, clear, serene, radiant atmosphere of Thy presence,
that there I may breathe freely, there repose in Thy love,
there be at rest from myself and from all things that weary me;
thence return, arrayed with Thy peace, to do and bear what shall please Thee.[9]

> Our labor should be to maintain unbroken
> communion with our blessed Lord; then we shall

have entire rest, and God abiding in us;
that which we do will not be ours, but His.

—John Kenneth Mackenzie

May 7

David's life is rich with conquests and struggles. He was a mighty king whose personal life became entangled with sin, including the adultery with Bathsheba, and his order to have her husband killed in battle so that he might cover up his egregious act.

The Bible tells it like it is with this giant of a man. He is one of the greatest men in the Old Testament. Yet his failures are on display for us. Why? It allows us to us to see that King David, God's chosen, was imperfect—a sinner. Yet God refers to Him as "a man after My heart" (Acts 13:22, NKJV).

David suffered consequences that stayed with him the rest of his life. God took the son born to him and Bathsheba. His son Absalom incited a widespread rebellion against him in order to seize his throne.

David was quick to tell God he was sorry for his sins. His repentance is seen in his plea for mercy and forgiveness in Psalm 51:

> Be gracious to me, O God...wash me and cleanse
> me... I have sinned against You...purify me, O
> God! Hide Your face from my sins...create a clean
> heart in me...restore me with joy...sustain me with
> a willing spirit...O Lord! Open my lips to declare
> Your praise.

We are born as sinners with natural instincts that portray our selfishness and indulgences in the things of the flesh. Let our hearts cry out as David's did.

Sinner that I am, Lord, I come before You with a contrite heart. Forgive me and restore me. I too am "after Your heart."

May 8

> The God of peace will soon crush Satan under your
> feet. May the grace of our Lord Jesus be with you.
>
> —Romans 16:20, NLT

I have known peace and joy the last while. I tell others of the blessings which You have lavishly supplied. I have been free of worry.

Yet today I awoke downtrodden, weary, and teary, unable to settle the thoughts of concern and worry. I am being attacked, and I know it. I recognized his work right away.

He tempts me with doubt and robs me of trust. He nags at my joyful spirit, drawing me into a place I fiercely resist.

O Lord, I know I never have to be afraid or discouraged. You are my God, and You will not allow me to fall. Satan looks for the opportunity to crush peace and joy, faith, hope, and trust. Discouragement and fear are two of his powerful weapons.

But You, O Lord, squelch his hold on me.

We can come into His presence where we experience peace and joy in our heart

All praise and honor to You, our Lord and our God. You have conquered Satan and rescued us from his tenacious grip.

May 9

> God created man in His own image.
>
> —Genesis 1:27, NASB

Child, think about your tongue. Do you realize if you could control it, you would be able to control yourself in every other way?

Man can tame animals, but no one can tame the tongue. It is restless and evil, full of deadly poison. Sometimes it praises Me, and sometimes it curses Me. Blessing and cursing come pouring out of your mouth (James 3:7, NLT).

Does a fountain give fresh and bitter water from its opening? What springs from your mouth often reflects who you are.

Does a fig tree produce olives or a grapevine produce figs?

I have made you in My image, and I can change you from the inside out. I will purify your heart, and you will hold your tongue.

When your heart is on fire for Me, your tongue will only send out blessings. (James 3:7–10, NLT)

Hold your tongue!

May 10

Sometimes something clicks, and with a tear, remembrance of the pain and the loneliness flood the heart.

Sometimes something clicks, and with a smile, remembrance of love and laughter flood the senses.

And there are times where nothing clicks at all, and a voice echoes through the emptiness and numbness, never finding the person who used to fill that space.

And sometimes—the most special times of all—a feeling ripples through your body, heart, and soul that tells you that person never left you, and she's right there with you through it all. (Unknown)

May 11

I was a young mother when I began to memorize scripture. It was a challenge, so I began with baby steps.

I approached it with the same formula I used when required to memorize something in school. I used word pictures and made up ridiculously funny things that would take root in my mind. I wanted to plant the scripture there and believed it would find its way to my heart. It did.

I use memorized scripture verses so much that if they were written each time I recite one, the pages would be worn and tattered.

It's a sure way of replacing the harassing thoughts that attempt to bring me down. Worry has no room in my day; I stamp it out with God's Word.

Sometimes without notice, a scripture springs from within, delighting my spirit.

"Ah Lord God! Behold, You have made the heavens and the earth by Your great power and by Your outstretched arm! Nothing is too difficult for You" (Jer. 32:17, NASB).

I cling to them when I am needy. "I can do all things through Him who strengthens me" (Phil. 4:13, NASB).

When I might be irritated with someone or something, "Set a guard, O LORD, over my mouth; keep watch over the door of my lips" (Ps. 141:3, NASB).

When unable to sleep, "In peace I will both lie down and sleep, For You alone, O Lord, make me to dwell in safety" (Ps. 4:8, NASB).

Memorizing scripture fills our head and heart leaving room for only Him.

May 12

> Who then will condemn us? No one—for Christ
> Jesus died for us and was raised to life for us, and
> He is sitting in the place of honor at God's right
> hand, pleading for us.
>
> —Romans 8:34, NLT

Victor Frankl was a prisoner in Hitler's concentration camps. He tells of his observation that "although every prisoner suffered the same inhumane conditions, some manage to hold on to their 'self' better than others…that sort of person the prisoner became, was the result of an inner decision and not the result of outer circumstances… everything can be taken from a man but one thing; the last of the human freedoms—to choose one's attitude in any given set of circumstances, to choose one's own way."

Can anything ever separate us from Christ's love? Does it mean He no longer loves us if we have trouble or calamity, or are persecuted, or hungry, or destitute, or in danger, or threatened with death?

No, despite all these things, overwhelming victory is ours through Christ, who loved us (Rom. 8:35–37, NLT).

May 13

> The eternal God is your Refuge, and His
> everlasting arms are under you…
>
> —Deuteronomy 33:27, NLT

I will pay attention to what You say and will listen carefully to Your words. I won't lose sight of them as I let them penetrate deep into my heart. They bring me life and heal my whole body.

I will guard my heart above all else, for I know it determines the course of my life.

I will avoid all perverse talk and stay away from corrupt speech.

I am determined to look straight ahead and fix my eyes on what lies ahead.

I mark out a straight path and stay on it because it is safe.

I will not get sidetracked and will keep my feet from following evil.

I will do all of this by Your power and strength, for I rely only on You and not on myself (Prov. 4:20–27, NLT).

> Not by might nor by power, but by My Spirit,
> says the Lord Almighty.
>
> —Zechariah 4:6, NKJV

I lay my head upon Thy infinite heart,
I hide beneath the shelter of Thy wing;
Pursued and tempted, helpless I must cling
To Thee, My Father;
Bid me not depart,
For sin and death pursue,
And life is where Thou art! (Anonymous)

May 14

As Jesus continued on toward Jerusalem, He reached the border between Galilee and Samaria.

As He entered a village there, ten lepers stood at a distance, crying out, "Jesus, Master, have mercy on us!"

He looked at them and said, "Go show yourselves to the priests." And as they went, they were cleansed of their leprosy.

One of them, when he saw that he was healed, came back to Jesus, shouting, "Praise God!" He fell to the ground at Jesus' feet, thanking Him for what He had done. This man was a Samaritan.

Jesus asked, "Didn't I heal ten men? Where are the other nine?" (Luke 17:11–17, NLT)

If a leper thought his disease was gone, he was to go to the priest, who could declare him clean. Jesus told these men to go to the priests *before* He cured them. And they went! Is our faith in God so strong that we will ask and trust before we see any evidence of an answer?

Jesus, Master, have mercy on us!

> Live by every word that comes
> from the mouth of the Lord.
>
> —Deuteronomy 8:3, NLT

May 15

> For the eyes of the Lord move to and fro
> throughout the earth that He may strongly support
> those whose heart is completely His.
>
> —2 Chronicles 16:9, NASB

O Lord, Your eyes search the whole earth in order to strengthen those whose hearts are fully committed to You. Such knowledge is inconceivable to me.

You are a shield around me;

You are my glory, the One who holds my head high.

My heart is confident in You, O God; no wonder I can sing praises with all my heart.

I meet this day confident of Your presence in every moment, singing songs of joy in my heart, for I know You are with me. Whatever You send, whatever You withhold, I will give You the honor and the glory.

Thank you!

> Worship is the highway of reverence and
> washes the dust of earth from our eyes.
>
> —Unknown

May 16

> I will hold you up with My victorious right hand.
>
> —Isaiah 41:10, NLT

Use thy utmost endeavor to attain such a disposition of spirit that thou mayest become one with Me.

And thy will may become so entirely conformed to My all-perfect will, that not only shalt thou never desire that which is evil, but not even that which is good, if it be not according to My will.

So that whatever shall befall thee in this earthly life, from whatsoever quarter it may come, whether in things temporal or things spiritual, nothing shall ever disturb thy peace, or trouble thy quietness of spirit.

But thou shalt be established in a firm belief that I, thine Omnipotent God, love thee with a dearer love and take of thee more watchful care than though canst for thyself.[10]

May 17

> Blessed is the one whose transgressions are
> forgiven, whose sins are covered.
>
> —Psalm 32:1, NLT

Child, you know the sin you have committed. Your conscience and your heart know. I want you to tell Me about it, to confess.

Do that, and I promise I will forgive you. I will wash you whiter than snow.

There will be no mention of it again, and you will be purified.

All I ask of you is that you confess, are heartily sorry, and resolve never to do it again.

I am just and faithful to forgive your sins and cleanse you from all unrighteousness.[11]

You will know joy when you experience forgiveness. When your sin is put out of sight, you are cleared of all guilt, and your life will be lived in complete honesty.

Yes, it is that simple. I cherish a contrite heart.

> One thing alone, dear Lord! I dread;
> To have a secret spot
> That separates my soul from Thee
> And yet to know it not. (Frederick W. Faber)

May 18

Our perishable bodies are subject to suffering, but Our Father never abandons us. Through the suffering and the pain, in the midst of overwhelming trials, He is always with us.

Jesus, You are the Light in the darkness, and Your light shines in my heart. That is why it is so clear to me that my power is from You. I am pressed on every side by troubles, but I am not crushed.

I am perplexed, but not driven to despair. You never abandon me.

I get knocked down, but I am not destroyed.

It is through suffering that my body continues to share in Your death so that the treasure of Your light may be seen in me (2 Cor. 4:7–10, NLT).

Yes, it is Your power that shines, enabling me to survive all that happens.

Thank You, Jesus.

May 19

> My future is in Your hands.
>
> —Psalm 31:15, NLT

For years I wondered why the Lord gave one of my older sisters, along with my younger sister, an artistic gift, and left me out. It was only when I let go of the question *why* and turned it over to God that He gave me peace about it. By His grace, I was able to take delight in my sisters' talents and their work.

Three days after my husband's twenty-ninth birthday, we knew something was seriously wrong with Bob, and I rushed him to the hospital. He couldn't turn his head.

That was the last time he walked on his own. After a five-and-a-half month hospital stay, he was able to walk with crutches. He could no longer work as a machinist, but the Lord provided for us until I could go to work. Bob has never complained about his disability.

Ever so slowly with no fanfare, the Lord's will for my life became perfectly clear. Because of our financial circumstances, I went to work and was able to use the business training and skills which He had given me.

We'll soon be eighty-eight. We have found that with faith and trust we are assured of God's hand in all things, even when our lives turn upside down and the future looks bleak. (Eva Wagner)

I have learned that faith means trusting in advance what will only make sense in reverse.

—Phillip Yancey

May 20

Child, I don't promise you that there won't be deep waters or that there won't be fire. I cannot protect you from those circumstances of life that befall mankind.

But I do promise you that you won't drown, and you won't be burned. For I will be with you through it all.

The water may be deep, the fire may appear to be all consuming, but you must know that I am there with you (Isa. 43:2, NLT).

Do you know that without a doubt?

If you look beyond Me for help or try to do it on your own, I cannot promise you that the water will not overflow or that you won't be scorched and burned.

Remember. You need Me, and I am here.

> Live by every word that comes
> from the mouth of the Lord.

—Deuteronomy 8:3

May 21

> Praise the Lord; praise God our Savior!
> For each day He carries us in His arms.

—Psalm 68:19, NLT

You are my Redeemer. You are the Lord my God, who teaches me what is good for me and leads me along the paths I should follow.

So I wait quietly before You, for my victory comes from You. You alone are my rock and my salvation, my fortress where I will never be shaken.

Everything I have or will ever have comes from You. There is nothing I claim as my own. I need to stop clinging to what I ultimately can't hold anyway.

Your Word gives me reason not to attempt possession of even today or tomorrow.

Look here, you who say, "Today or tomorrow we are going to a certain town and will stay there a year. We will do business there and make a profit."

How do you know what your life will be like tomorrow? Your life is like the morning fog—it's here a little while, then it's gone. What you ought to say is, "If the Lord wants us to, we will live and do this or that" (James 4:13–15, NLT),

Help me to hold lightly those things of this world. Open my mind and heart to always recognize that You are the foundation on which I can build my life.

I wait quietly before You, for my victory comes from You.

May 22

> Lord, give me Your unfailing love.
>
> —Psalm 119:41, NLT

Child, I never tire of caring for you. Even when you don't feel Me, I am here with you. I am as close to you as the breath you take. I understand your heartaches and disappointments. When you stumble, I grab you. When you fall, I lift you up. You cannot comprehend My love for you.

There is nothing that will ever separate us.

When others judge you, I am your defense.

When you are in pain, your health in jeopardy, I am your physician.

When you are sad, I am your joy.

When you weep, I dry your tears.

When afraid, I will hold you. Do not worry or fret.

You are Mine, and I am here with you.

> How sweet Your words taste to me;
> they are sweeter than honey.
>
> —Psalm 119:103, NLT

May 23

> I am the Way, the Truth, and the Life. No
> one can come to the Father except through
> Me. If you had really known Me, you would
> know who My Father is. From now on,
> you do know Him and have seen Him!
>
> —John 14:6–7, NLT

Philip said, "Lord, show us the Father, and we will be satisfied."

Jesus replied, "Have I been with you all this time, Philip, and yet you still don't know who I am? Anyone who has seen Me has seen the Father! So why are you asking Me to show Him to you? Don't you believe that I am in the Father and the Father is in Me? The words I speak are not My own, but My Father who lives in Me does His work through Me. Just believe that I am in the Father, and the Father is in Me. Or at least believe because of the work you have seen Me do" (John 14:8–11, NLT).

If we know Jesus, we know the Father!

> Heaven and earth will disappear, but My words
> will never disappear.
>
> —Matthew 24:35, NLT

May 24

> Give Me your burdens and I will take care of you.
> I will not permit you to slip.
>
> —Psalm 5:22, NLT

Lord, when I cast my burdens on You, I am free of all matters that weigh me down. I am lifted above the cares that press upon my mind and heart.

I feel like a child with no worries or cares, knowing of the security of my parent, who sees to my every need. I slip now into Your arms knowing that You will take care of me, and I am free to love and serve You.

There is no circumstance, no trouble, no testing,
that can ever touch me until, first of all, it has gone
past God and past Christ, right through to me. If it
has come that far, it has come with a great purpose.

—Alan Redpath

May 25

And this is the plan: At the right time He will
bring everything together under the authority of
Christ—everything in heaven and on earth.

—Ephesians 1:10, NLT

Father, You saved me by Your grace when I believed. I can't take credit, for this is Your gift to me. Salvation is not a reward for the good things I have done; I certainly can't boast about it.

I rely on Your power, O God. You are perfect, not changeable like me. Ground me, plant my feet so deeply in You that I will not move. If left on my own, I stray.

I am caught up by distractions and concerns. Oh, yes, I am fickle. But I will stand firmly in this place, trusting in You, my perfect God.

You are sovereign and in charge of all that happens to me. When my life seems chaotic, I rest in this truth. Your purpose to save me cannot be thwarted no matter what evil Satan may bring.

Praise You, Father!

May 26

When she was six weeks old, as the result of a doctor's careless error she was afflicted with lifelong blindness.

Frances Jane Crosby wrote, "It seemed intended by the blessed Providence of God that I should be blind all my life, and I thank Him for the dispensation."

Fanny considered her blindness to be one of her greatest blessings. She accepted it as a gift from God. "I could not have written thousands of hymns," she said, "if I had been hindered by the distractions of seeing all the interesting and beautiful objects that would have been presented to my notice."

Her first poem, written when she was eight years old, reflects her perspective until her death at ninety-five.

> Oh, what a happy child I am,
> Although I cannot see!
> I am resolved that in this world
> Contended I will be.
> How many blessings I enjoy
> That other people don't!

> So weep or sigh that I am blind,
> I cannot, nor I won't!

Fanny wrote eight thousand songs, among them "To God Be the Glory," "Blessed Assurance," "Redeemed," and "All the Way My Savior Leads Me."

Have we forgotten how to be grateful? The example of Fanny, a blind hymn writer, seems extraordinary. And it is!

May 27

Heavenly Father, You assure me that You began a good work within me, and You will continue that work until it is finally finished on the day Your Son, Jesus, returns.

I will not throw away my confident trust in You. I will remember the great reward it brings me!

Holy, holy, holy, Lord God the Almighty; the One Who always was, Who is and Who is still to come! Alleluia! (Rev. 4:8,11, NLT)

You are worthy, O Lord my God, to receive glory, and honor, and power. For You created all things, and they exist because You created what You pleased.

I know that patient endurance is what I need now so that I will continue to do Your will. Then I will receive all that You have promised.

May 28

> God called to him from the middle of the bush,
> "Moses! Moses!"
>
> —Exodus 3:4, NLT

Moses was a man to whom God spoke directly. He literally heard the voice of God, who said of Moses, "With him I speak mouth to mouth." When people had a question, Moses said, "I'll go ask God." He went to God in prayer and expected an answer.

It was that simple for Moses. He had come to rely totally on God for his every need. His relationship with God was that of a father and son.

When I was young mother, I began to attend women's Bible study. One verse that caught my attention was "Never stop praying." I believed that was a command that I couldn't achieve. It was for the monks nestled in their monastery who had nothing to do but pray. The demands on my time limited the time on my knees.

But studying the Bible with others became a priority. And the more I learned, the more I wanted to learn. I had grown up with ritual prayer, so talking personally to God was unfamiliar to me

I began talking to Him, keeping it simple. "I love you, Jesus." I disciplined myself to say it often. And the more I said it, the more I knew it!

My prayer life began to grow. In the company of others, doing household chores, driving kids here and there, in the checkout line, "I love you, Jesus!" would spring from within and settle in my thoughts. I never stopped praying.

I call it my arrow prayer. *Webster* defines *arrow* as "any of various things that resemble an arrow in shape, function, or speed, such as a sign indicating direction or position." My prayer was aimed directly to God.

I'm grateful for the Bible studies that have continued to give me scriptural verses, which I apply to my spiritual growth, resulting in never-ending prayer.

> The ultimate goal of Bible study is application,
> not interpretation.
>
> —Rick Warren

May 29

Teach me Your ways, O Lord that I may live according to Your truth. Grant me purity of heart so that I may honor You. With all my heart I will praise You, O Lord my God.

I will give glory to Your name forever, for Your love for me is very great (Ps. 86:11–13, NLT).

You are my Sun and my Shield. You give me grace and glory. You will withhold no good thing from those of us who do what is right. O Lord of Heaven's Armies, what joy for those who trust in You! (Ps. 84:11–12, NLT)

> Joy is prayer. Joy is strength. Joy is love. Joy is a net
> of love by which you can catch souls.
>
> —Mother Teresa

May 30

Father, You love me so much that You sent Your Son, Jesus, to die for me that I would have eternal life. Such knowledge is too wonderful to me. As I ponder this kind of love and sacrifice, I ask You, how can You love one such as me? I am unworthy and frayed in every way. Yet Your Word is filled with such love.

> My heart leaps with joy at the wonder.
> I put all my hope in You, Lord.
> You are my Helper, my Shield.
> My heart rejoices for I trust in Your holy name.

Let Your unfailing love surround me, for my hope is
in You alone. (Ps. 33:20–22, NLT)

Trusting God's grace means trusting God's love
for us rather than our love for God. Therefore,
our prayers should consist mainly of rousing our
awareness of God's love for us rather than trying to
rouse God's awareness of our love for Him.

—Peter Kreeft

May 31

I give all praise to You, O God, Father of my Lord, Jesus,
who has blessed me with every spiritual blessing in the
heavenly realms because I am united with Christ.

Even before You made the world, You loved me and
chose me in Christ to be holy and without fault in Your eyes.

You decided in advance to adopt me into Your family by
bringing me to You through Jesus. This is what You wanted
to do, and it gave You great pleasure.

So I praise You God for the glorious grace You have
poured out on me.

You are so rich in kindness and grace that You purchased
my freedom with the blood of Your Son and forgave my
sins (Eph. 1:3–8, NLT).

You have showered Your kindness on me, along with all wisdom and understanding.

Praise You, My Lord and My God!

June 1

> But you belong to God, my dear children. You have already won a victory over those people, because the Spirit who lives in you is greater than the spirit who lives in the world.
>
> —1 John 4:4, NLT

Why is it that we, in the very kingdom of grace, surrounded by angels, and preceded by saints, nevertheless can do so little, and, instead of mounting with wings like eagles, we grovel in the dust, and do but sin, and confess sin alternately?

What we lack is the simple, earnest, sincere inclination and aim to use what God has given us, and what we have in us.[12]

God is on my side. He makes Himself responsible for my being. If I will only entrust myself to Him with the cordial return of trustful love, than all that He has breathed into my heart of human possibility, He will realize and bring to perfection. (Charles Gore)

June 2

I know that if I sin, I have an advocate, one who is truly righteous. Lord Jesus, You plead my case before the Father. Your Word assures me that You are the sacrifice that atones for my sins, not just mine, but the sins of the whole world (1 John 2:1–2, NASB).

I rely on Your promise that I will truly know You if I obey Your commandments. In doing so, it shows how much I love you. And by my obedience, I know that I am living in Your will.

May my life reflect that love in all I do or say. And by knowing and obeying Your commandments, I will be free from the bondage of sin.

Even though my human nature gives in to sin, I will be free from Satan's grip and know that You defend me before the Father.

All glory to You Lord Jesus, now and forever.

> The grass withers and the flowers fade, but the
> Word of our God stands forever.
>
> —Isaiah 40:8, NLT

June 3

> Faith is the confidence that what we hope for will
> actually happen; it gives us assurance about things
> we cannot see.
>
> —Hebrews 11:1, NLT

I understand that it is impossible to please You without faith. So I come to you with the firm belief that You exist and will reward me when I sincerely seek You.

I rely on Your Word, which is alive and powerful. I know it is sharper than the sharpest two-edged sword.

Jesus, I proclaim You are the King of kings and Lord of lords. Who can I name with such power and prestige that I need only call upon and am ushered in? Would it be kings or presidents? No!

You are the God of the universe and invite me to desire You. Oh, yes, Lord, I come to be in the radiance of Your presence, to worship and adore You.

June 4

As Jesus was starting out on His way to Jerusalem, a man came running up to Him, knelt down, and asked, "Good Teacher, what must I do to inherit eternal life?"

"Why do you call Me good?" Jesus asked. "Only God is truly good. But to answer your question, you know the commandments: You must not murder. You must not commit adultery. You must not steal. You must not testify falsely. You must not cheat anyone. Honor your father and mother."

"Teacher," the man replied, "I've obeyed all these commandments since I was young."

Looking at the man, Jesus felt genuine love for him. "There is still one thing you haven't done," He told him. "Go and sell all your possessions and give the money to the poor, and you will have treasure in heaven. Then come, follow Me."

At this the man's face fell, and he went away sad, for he had many possessions.

Jesus looked around and said to His disciples, "How hard it is for the rich to enter the Kingdom of God!" This amazed them.

But Jesus said again, "Dear children, it is very hard to enter the Kingdom of God. In fact, it is easier for a camel to go through the eye of a needle than for a rich person to enter the Kingdom of God!"

The disciples were astounded. "Then who in the world can be saved?" they asked.

Jesus looked at them intently and said, "Humanly speaking, it is impossible, but not with God. Everything is possible with God" (Mark 10:17–27, NLT).

> Does not My Word burn like fire? Is it not like a
> mighty hammer that smashes a rock to pieces?
>
> —Jeremiah 23:29, NLT

June 5

> There is no truth in him [the devil].
>
> —John 8:44, NLT

Listen to my prayer, gracious Lord. You are my Helper and have brought me through many trials. You lift me when I fall and catch me when I stumble. I know You love me and can do all things.

These times of discouragement are the attacks of the enemy. I rush to You for rescue. Satan slips in, trying to distract me. He delights when I am discouraged and troubled. But You are the Mighty God and have dominion over him. I trust in You.

Hear me as I pray; listen to my voice in the morning. Walk with me this day.

I will praise You with all my heart knowing that whatever Your plans are for me, they are of Your design. You will conquer all that interferes with our sweet communion. You have overcome Satan, and victory is Yours!

For every child of God defeats this evil world, and we achieve this victory through our faith.

—1 John 5:4, NLT

June 6

These words of Peter deserve our attention:

> I want to remind you that in the last days, scoffers will come, mocking the truth and following their own desires. They will say, "What happened to the promise that Jesus is coming again? From before the times of our ancestors, everything has remained the same since the world was first created."
>
> But you must not forget this one thing, dear friends, a day is like a thousand years to the Lord, and a thousand years is like a day. The Lord isn't really being slow about His promise, as some people think. No, He is being patient for your sake. He does not want anyone to be destroyed, but wants everyone to repent.
>
> But the day of the Lord will come as unexpectedly as a thief. Then the heavens will pass away with a terrible noise, and the very elements themselves

will disappear in fire, and the earth and everything on it will be found to deserve judgment.

Since everything around us is going to be destroyed like this, what holy and godly lives you should live, looking forward to the day of God and hurrying it along. On that day, He will set the heavens on fire, and the elements will melt away in the flames.

We are looking forward to the new heavens and new earth He has promised, a world filled with God's righteousness.

And so, dear friends, while you are waiting for these things to happen, make every effort to be found living peaceful lives that are pure and blameless in His sight. (2 Pet. 3:3–14, NLT)

June 7

Child, I am the Lord; there is no other God.
I create the light and make the darkness.
I send good times and bad times.
I, the Lord, am the One who does these things.
Open up, O heavens, and pour out your righteousness.
Let the earth open wide so salvation and
righteousness can sprout up together.

I, the Lord, created them.
What sorrow awaits those who argue with their Creator.
Does a clay pot argue with its maker?
Does the clay dispute with the one who shapes it, saying,
"Stop, you're doing it wrong!"
Does the pot exclaim, "How clumsy
can you be?" (Isa. 45:5–9, NLT)

> Commit yourself wholeheartedly
> to these words of Mine.
>
> —Deuteronomy 11:18, NLT

June 8

> And so, dear brothers and sisters, I plead with
> you to give your bodies to God because of all He
> has done for you. Let them be a living and holy
> sacrifice—the kind He will find acceptable. This is
> truly the way to worship Him.
>
> —Romans 12:1, NLT

I want to give myself to You because of all that You have done for me. My desire is to be a living and holy sacrifice that You find acceptable. I want to worship You.

Your Word gives me direction. It instructs me to bless those who persecute me. I am not to curse them but pray for Your blessings on them.

I am to be happy with those who are happy and weep with those who weep. You ask that I live in harmony with everyone. And I'm not to think I know it all! (Rom. 12:14–17, NLT)

Your Word convicts me to never be proud and not to consider myself better than others. It tells me I must do all I can to live in peace with everyone, don't take revenge, but leave it to You, my righteous God.

I am to feed my enemies if they are hungry and give them drink if they thirst (Rom. 12:20, NLT).

These are challenging directives, Lord. I am grateful that You assure me all things are possible with You. I cling to that promise, for only by Your grace will I be able to fulfill my desire to be a holy and living sacrifice, pleasing to You.

June 9

> My soul *waits* for the Lord. More than those who watch for the morning.
>
> —Psalm 130:6, NASB

I was a poor patient. I had open heart surgery, and I knew the healing process would take some time. But I didn't realize *how* long!

Initially I was hopeful, but as the weeks went by, I became an impatient patient! I exhausted the means of distractions that I had originally engaged in while appreciating the free time to sit and heal. But I was tired of reading, e-mails, and Internet; time to start moving. I felt like I was creeping up an endless flight of stairs, and I wanted an elevator!

William Ullathorne writes, "Trials of mind affect us more deeply than pains of body, and if we give in to anxiety, such trials become troubles and are immensely increased."

He's right. The soul that rests in calm endurance experiences healing, which in turn increases the ability of the body to heal. I needed to be reminded that I had entrusted myself into God's care and was now doubting. I had looked away.

We can be such fragile and weak children. Only our Father, in His powerful love, can look with compassion on our feebleness. In due time, He will guide us back, showing us the blessedness of waiting on Him and not on ourselves or our bodies.

> For if Christ be born within,
> Soon that likeness shall appear
> Which the soul had lost through sin.
> God's own image fair and clear,

And the soul serene and bright
Mirror back His heavenly light. (Laurentius Laurenti)

June 10

I step out on the back deck. The sunrise, displayed in shades of pink, splashes across the baby blue sky. All is still. From the heavens and on earth the day has sprung alive!

Sing a new song to the LORD! Let the whole earth sing to the LORD!

Sing to the LORD, bless His Name (Ps. 96:1, NLT).

The LORD made the heavens, splendor and majesty are before Him, and strength and beauty are in His sanctuary (Ps. 96:6, NLT).

Let the heavens be glad and let the earth rejoice.

Let the sea and everything in it shout His praise! (Ps. 96:11, NLT)

I will exalt You, my Lord and God, and worship at Your footstool.

You are Holy!

The earth is the Lord's and all it contains.

June 11

Child, I bless those who are poor and realize their need for Me. The Kingdom of heaven is theirs.

I bless those who mourn, assuring them of My comfort.

I bless the humble, for they will inherit the whole earth.

I bless those who hunger and thirst for justice. They will be satisfied.

I bless those who are merciful. I will show them mercy. I bless the pure of heart, for they will see Me.

I bless those who work for peace. They will be called My children.

I bless those who are persecuted for doing right. The Kingdom of heaven is theirs.

I bless you when people mock you and persecute you, and lie about you, and say all sorts of evil things against you because you are My followers. Be happy about it when they do because a great reward awaits you in heaven (Matt. 5:3–12, NLT).

I bless you in all things that lead to Me. You are My child, and I love you.

Live by every word that comes
from the mouth of the Lord.

—Deuteronomy 8:3, NLT

June 12

> I thank Christ Jesus our Lord, who has given
> me strength to do His work. He considered me
> trustworthy and appointed me to serve Him.
>
> —1 Timothy 1:12, NLT

I will be glad in Your strength and rejoice in Your salvation.

You have given me my heart's desires and not withheld anything I have asked of You.

You bless me with good and crown me with Your goodness, which is as precious as gold to me.

I asked life of You, and You have given it to me, extending my length of days.

Through Your salvation, I have known abundant blessings.

I am joyful, filled to the brim with gladness in Your presence (Ps. 21:2–6, NASB).

Thank You for giving me the strength to do Your work. You have considered me trustworthy and have chosen me to serve You.

I am a sinner redeemed by Your blood and mercy. Oh, how generous and gracious You are! You have filled me with faith and love that can come only from You.

I want to imitate You in everything I do and to live a life filled with love following Your example. You love me and offered Yourself as a sacrifice for me, a pleasing aroma to God (Eph. 5:1–2, NLT).

June 13

> The Lord nurses them when they are
> sick and restores them to health.
>
> —Psalm 41:3, NLT

He is our hope in times of sickness, and it will bring us comfort to know that He promises to preserve our life.

Paul writes of this about his affliction:

> Therefore, in order to keep me from becoming conceited, I was given a thorn in my flesh, a messenger of Satan, to torment me. Three times I pleaded with the Lord to take it away from me. But He said to me, "My grace is sufficient for you, for My power is made perfect in weakness."
>
> For Christ's sake, I delight in weaknesses, in sickness and in difficulties. For when I am weak, then I am strong. (2 Cor. 12:7–11, NLT)

We don't know what was wrong with Paul. Whatever it was, he pleaded with God to remove it. But instead, God assured him that He would demonstrate His power in Paul. Weakness—whether physically or otherwise, it helps us to develop our character. By admitting our weakness, we confirm God's strength and not our own.

> He gives power to the weak, and to *those who have*
> no might He increases strength.
>
> —Isaiah 40:29, NKJV

June 14

Jesus, I know that God who raised You from the dead will also raise me and present me to Himself with You (2 Cor. 4:14, NLT).

Though my body is dying, my spirit is being renewed every day. For my present troubles are small and won't last very long. Yet they produce for me a glory that vastly outweighs them and will last forever.

So I don't look at the troubles I can see now; rather, I fix my gaze on things that cannot be seen. For the things I see now will soon be gone, but the things I cannot see will last forever! (2 Cor. 4:16–18, NLT)

God will not permit any troubles to come upon us, unless He has a specific plan by which great blessing can come out of the difficulty.

—Peter Marshall

June 15

Whatever you have learned or received or heard from me, or seen in me—put it into practice. And the God of peace will be with you.

—Philippians 4:9, NLT

I want to dedicate all I am to You. I want to live according to all You would have me to be.

Your love for me is inconceivable. Because of Your horrendous suffering and death, my sins are forgiven, and I have been redeemed by Your blood.

You are perfectly good and righteous.

I am fashioned in Your likeness and will fix my thoughts on what is true and honorable, right, pure, lovely, and admirable. I will think of things that are excellent and worthy of praise (Phil. 4:8, NLT).

You are elevated to the place of highest honor and a name above all other names. At Your name every knee should bow in heaven and on earth and under the earth, and every tongue confess that You are Lord, to the glory of God the Father (Phil. 2:9–11, NLT).

> Heaven and earth will disappear,
> but My words will never disappear.
>
> —Matthew 24:35, NLT

June 16

> As for me, I know that my Redeemer lives.
>
> —Job 19:25, NASB

I have asked God for things, and He has said, no. And I have asked Him, "Why not?"

He answers Job's "Why not?" question:

> Where were you when I laid the foundation of the
>   earth?
> Tell *Me*, if you have understanding
> Who set its measurements? Since you know.
> Or who stretched the line on it?
> On what were its bases sunk?
> Or who laid its cornerstone,
> When the morning stars sang together
> And all the sons of God shouted for joy?

Or *who* enclosed the sea with doors
When, bursting forth, it went out from the womb;
When I made a cloud its garment
And thick darkness its swaddling band, And I
    placed boundaries on it
And set a bolt and doors,
And I said, 'Thus far you shall come, but no farther;
And here shall your proud waves stop'? (Job 38:4–
    11, NASB; emphasis mine)

Standing on this bit of beach watching the waves stop where He has ordered, I see His mighty power at work. "Why" is replaced with "Thank You."

> I know that You can do all things, and that no
> purpose of Yours can be thwarted!
>
> —Job 42:2, NASB

June 17

Overheard outside a concert hall:
    "What a singer! His voice filled the hall."
    "Yes, several of us had to leave the hall to make room for it!"
    Overheard in a spiritual counseling session:

"How can I love God as the scriptures tell us to? How can I give Him my whole heart?"

"You must first empty your heart of all created things."

Misleading! Don't be afraid to fill your heart with the people and things you love, for the love of God won't occupy space in your heart any more than a singer's voice occupies space in a concert hall.

Love is not like a loaf of bread. If I give a chunk of the loaf to you, I have less to offer to others.

You can love your mother, and your husband or wife, and each of your children with your whole heart. The wonder is that giving the whole of it to one person does not force you to give less to another.

On the contrary, each one of them now gets more. For if you love only your friend and no one else, it is a feeble heart that you offer. Your friend would stand to gain if you also give it to others.[13]

June 18

> Oh, the joys of those who trust the Lord.
>
> —Psalm 40:4, NLT

You are gracious and just.

You shower me with abundant compassion, loving me so much that You call me blessed because I long for You.

Such a great and mighty God You are!

You sent Your Son to earth, longing to draw all men to You.

He healed the sick, gave sight to the blind, and raised the dead.

In the end, He shed His precious blood that I might have eternal life.

Such love I cannot comprehend.

You know the longings of my heart, O God.

Lavish me with Your love; pour sweet fragrance over me that my soul will be pleasing to You.

Bathe me in the luxury of Your righteousness.

I am Yours, and You are mine.

June 19

> Lord, to whom would we go?
>
> —John 6:68, NLT

Child, many disciples didn't believe in Me. Things I said didn't make sense in their minds because they were steeped in laws and customs and Jewish traditions. They chose not to follow.

Even the twelve who followed Me were baffled by My teaching. "Are you going to leave Me also?" I asked them. "But Lord," Peter said, "to whom would we go? You have the words that give eternal life. We do believe, and we know You are the Holy One of God" (John 6:68–69, NLT).

Although they didn't understand everything I told them, they couldn't turn and walk away. They couldn't go back to their lives once they had found Me. They couldn't go back to their fishing boats or return to being a tax collector, pilfering from fellow Jews. Impossible!

Is it the same for you? You have found Me and know Me. Even though you don't understand everything, isn't it impossible to turn and follow your old ways?

Stay, and I will continue to teach you. We will be inseparable.

June 20

Elkanah had two wives. One bore him children, but Hannah, whom he loved, was unable to conceive.

Having numerous children was a status symbol, and Hannah considered herself a failure. A husband was permitted to divorce a barren wife, but Elkanah loved her and didn't want to part from her.

Hannah prayed for years that God would give her a child. She vowed, "If you give me a son, I will dedicate him to You all the days of his life."

She conceived and gave birth to a son, Samuel. When she had weaned him (at probably about five years old) she took him to Eli, the priest. "Sir, do you remember me?" Hannah asked. "I am the very woman who stood here several years ago praying to the LORD. I asked the LORD to give me this boy, and He has granted my request. Now I am giving him to the LORD, and he will belong to the LORD his whole life" (1 Sam. 1:26–28, NLT).

This is a story of God's answer to prayer. Hannah was filled with praise and trust in God's sovereignty.

"No one is holy like the LORD! There is no one besides You; there is no Rock like our God" (1 Sam. 2:2, NLT).

No doubt it was heartwrenching to leave this beautiful little boy and return to an empty house, but by faith, Hannah followed through on her promise and trusted God for the outcome.

In the years that followed, Hannah visited Samuel regularly. She and Elkanah had three others sons and two daughters.

I want that kind of faith, Lord. I dedicate those I love to You. I leave them with You, and I trust You for the outcome.

June 21

Almighty God, You are not man so You do not lie. You are not human so You do not change Your mind. When You have spoken You have never failed to act. And when You promise, You carry it through (Num. 23:19, NLT).

You are faithful, keeping Your covenant for a thousand generations, lavishing Your unfailing love on me because I love You and seek to obey You (Deut. 7:9, NLT).

You promise that even if a mother feels no love for her child—if she forgets her nursing child—You will never forget me. You have written my name on the palm of Your hand (Isa. 49:15–16, NLT).

You are a mighty Savior and take delight in me with gladness. With Your love, You calm all my fears and rejoice over me with joyful songs (Zeph. 3:17, NLT).

Such knowledge is too wonderful to me. You are the Almighty God who was, and is, and is to come!

June 22

> The steadfast of mind You will keep in perfect
> peace, because he trusts in You.
>
> —Isaiah 26:3, NASB

We live in a wooded area in the South that is the home to many of God's creatures—raccoons among them. They may look cute but are mischievous and destructive, so we set traps and take them to an unpopulated area and release them.

It's break of dawn, and I am here in my time with the Lord. Outside I hear the gnawing and clawing of a raccoon that is trapped, trying to escape. I know the only way it will be set free is when my husband takes it and releases it.

I am feeling like that raccoon: trapped. I long for release from this pain for my loved ones, buried so deep that I cannot express it. I think back on events that have brought me here. The seeds of choices that were planted through the years have rooted and produced fruit, good and bad.

The tears flow silently; my heart cracks without a sound. My soul twists and turns within. And I cry out, "Touch me, Lord. Release me!"

Just as the raccoon must wait for Ed to release him, so I wait on You, my Savior, to break the snare holding me captive.

As Your Spirit moves within me, I begin to feel the perfect peace, that You promise.

My heart finds joy in Psalm 25:15 (NIV), "My eyes are ever on the LORD, for only He will release my feet from the snare."

The circumstances aren't different, Lord. But I am. Because of the hope of the Gospel, my faith is grounded in knowing that You are sovereign. You have control of everything, and I can rest in You.

I choose today to trust You with my loved ones, and when I do, I know the sweet release of Your

peace is mine, because my mind stays on You.
(Barbara Cingoranelli)

June 23

> There was no room for them in the inn.
>
> —Luke 2:7

Henry Drummond says that the soul, in its highest sense, is a vast capacity for God.

It is like a curious chamber added on to being, and somehow involving being.

It is like a chamber with elastic and contractile walls, which can be expanded, with God as its guest, illimitably.

But, which without God, shrinks and shrivels until every vestige of the Divine is gone.

> By rooting out our selfish desires, even when
> they appear to touch no one but ourselves, we are
> preparing a chamber of the soul where the Divine
> Presence may dwell.
>
> —Ellen Watson

June 24

O God, to You be all the glory. By Your mighty power at work within me You are able to accomplish infinitely more than I can even think or ask. I am so foolish when I try to fix those things over which I have no control. I leave You out.

When I exhaust all possibilities to resolve them myself, I turn to You. You can do all things and meet all my needs according to Your glorious riches in Your Son, Jesus.

And so I am determined that I will rejoice in confident hope and patience in trouble.

I will continue to pray and be thankful in all circumstances, for I know this is Your will for me; I belong to You.

I will not worry about anything but instead pray about everything.

I will always tell You what I need and always be thankful for what You have done.

I will meet the future confident of Your protection. No matter what may happen, I am armored with grace for whatever comes my way.

I will not allow fear or anxiety to dictate my life.

I will pause in those moments, recenter myself, and find Your divine grace, replacing those moments with Your peace.

June 25

> For God so loved the world, that He gave His only begotten Son, that whoever believes in Him shall not perish, but have eternal life.
>
> —John 3:16, NASB

I have gone to church all of my life.

It makes me think of the story told of the young man who walked into the kitchen where his new bride was preparing Sunday dinner. He watched as she took the medium-sized ham, cut it in two, and put each half in a different pan. "Why are you cutting the ham in two and baking it in separate pans?" he asked. "I don't know," she said. "My mother did it that way."

Later, when she had the opportunity to ask her mother, her mother said, "I never had a pan big enough to bake the large ham required to feed our family. So I cut it in two and baked it in two smaller pans."

I suspect we have all done things a certain way without really understanding why and only because our mother or father did it that way. I think that's why I went to church. My parents did. And so I was exposed to the teachings of faith at a very young age.

I grew up believing in God and that Jesus is the Son of God.

I was taught that sin is any thought or action that violated His law. It's independence from God—turning away from Him and following our own stubborn will.

Because of our sinfulness, God sent a Savior, His Son, Jesus, to reconcile man to Himself. Jesus willingly suffered and died on the cross. He took responsibility for all our sins. When we believe that, are truly sorry for our sins, and ask forgiveness, He forgives us.

Jesus rose from the dead and ascended into heaven. He is a living God.

I was an adult when I made a commitment to a personal relationship with Jesus. When I did, gradually all those truths I had learned as a youngster became so real to me. I began to mature in the faith that had been planted in my heart as a child.

I am grateful for the foundation my parents provided that continues to lead me to spiritual maturity and a deep personal relationship with God.

June 26

> Bless the Lord, O my soul, and all that is within me, *bless* His holy name.
>
> —Psalm 103:1, NASB

Lord, I praise You with my whole heart. I praise Your holy blessed name. I will never forget all You have done for me.

Oh, the blessings are bountiful!

I thank You for all You have withheld from me.

You forgive my sins and crown me with love and tender mercies. Such knowledge is too wonderful for me; I cannot attain to it.

You know how weak I am, Lord Jesus, and You remember that I am only dust. My days on this earth are like the grass and wildflowers that bloom and die. The wind blows, and I am gone, as though I had never been here.

But I know Your love endures forever with those of us who fear You. Your salvation extends to my children's children (Ps. 103:17,19, NASB).

Yes, I praise You, Lord. The heavens are Your throne, and from there You rule. And one day I will be with You.

June 27

When Larry and I began attending a couples' Bible study, a love and appreciation for the Old Testament came alive for me. Our teacher Jack traced passages from Old Testament prophecy to fulfillment of them in the New Testament. Fascinating!

One example is found in Jeremiah 7:11 (NLT). "Don't you yourselves admit that this temple, which bears My name, has become a den of thieves? Surely I see all the evil going on there. I, the LORD, have spoken!

We read of Jesus clearing the temple in John 2:13–16 (NLT).

It was nearly time for the Jewish Passover celebration, so Jesus went to Jerusalem. In the Temple area He saw merchants selling cattle, sheep, and doves for sacrifices; He also saw dealers at tables exchanging foreign money. Jesus made a whip from some ropes and chased them all out of the Temple. He drove out the sheep and cattle, scattered the money changers' coins over the floor, and turned over their tables. Then, going over to the people who sold doves, He told them, "Get these things out of here. Stop turning My Father's house into a marketplace!"

We may read many books in our lifetime, but none compare to the Word of God, spoken and fulfilled.

Studying the Bible with others opens our hearts and minds on a journey of coming to know our God and Creator.

> One reason I love to study God's Word is the
> joyfulness that results in my spirit from new
> understandings that I gain through the application
> of God's Word to my life.
>
> —Sharon Steffen

June 28

> Be kind to each other, tender-hearted.
>
> —Ephesians 4:32, NASB

Deep tenderness of spirit is the very soul and marrow of the Christ-life. What specific gravity is to the planet, what beauty is to the rainbow, what perfume is to the rose, what marrow is to the bone, what rhythm is to poetry, what the pulse is to the heart, what harmony is to music, what heat is to the human body-all this, and much more is tenderness of spirit in religion.

It is possible to be very religious, and staunch and persevering in all Christian duties; possible even, to be sanctified, to be a brave defender and preacher of holiness, to be mathematically orthodox, and blameless in outward life, and very zealous in good works, and yet to be greatly lacking in tenderness of spirit-that all subduing, all melting love, which is the very cream and quintessence of Heaven, and which incessantly streamed out from the voice and eyes of the Blessed Jesus.[14]

Are we tenderhearted, moved quickly to compassion and pity for those who suffer and are in distress? Or is it easier to ignore the condition, feeling it doesn't affect us?

June 29

I am sitting at my desk editing. I am distracted by what's going on outside the window over my desk. I can hardly work while watching the mockingbird flying back and forth to feed her two babies that wait atop the red bougainvillea. They are calm in between courses, perched on top, patiently waiting. But then suddenly their high-pitched peeping and fluttering are signs that Mom is coming.

I review this particular devotional and can't help but compare this bird's care for her chicks to the care the Almighty Father lavishes on His children.

Psalm 91 instructs us that if we dwell in the shelter of the Most High, we will abide in the shadow of the Almighty.

It reminds us the Lord is our Refuge and our Fortress, our God, in whom we trust.

It assures us it is He who delivers us from the snare of the trapper and from the deadly pestilence.

It promises us He will cover us with His pinion, and under His wings we can seek refuge.

It guarantees us His faithfulness is a shield and bulwark.

He will give His angels charge concerning us and guard us in all our ways.

It is in His Word that we find the solution to all that can burden us and bring us down. We are safe with Him, for He supplies all we need.

June 30

How can we know if we are growing in our relationship with God, that we are maturing?

One sign we might look for is whether we maintain more calmness in the midst of the troubles that afflict us.

That we have peace of mind when steeped in all that used to distract us and agitate our soul.

We turn to God in prayer for everything.

We know that we are not controlled by our sinful nature but by the Spirit.

We recognize the difference in how we deal with burdens that once pulled us down. Now we find strength in Him.

We know without a doubt of His promise—that He will never fail nor abandon us.

Because we belong totally to Christ Jesus, we have nailed the passions and desires of our sinful nature to His cross and crucified them there (Gal. 5:24, NLT).

We were dead because of our sins. Then God made us alive with Christ, for He forgave all our sins. (I can do all things through Him who strengthens me.)

We are maturing, but we will never fully mature in our relationship with God.

It gives us joy in knowing that we strive for maturity in our spiritual growth and that He is pleased. One of these days, we will be with Him in heaven, and we will be all grown up!

July 1

> He humbled Himself by becoming obedient to the
> point of death, even death on a cross.
>
> —Philippians 2:8, NASB

It is impossible for us to imagine subjecting ourselves to death on a cross. But Christ did that for us. He was obedient to the point of death. I may not be asked to humble myself in obedience to the point of death, but God expects me to obey.

Do we really desire to obey God? Do we strive to obey with the exercise of small acts, attending to details of everyday duties, thinking of ourselves as a child who matures in obedience by learning what is expected of her? She experiences the rewards of obedience and the consequences of disobedience.

We must try to recognize a sin in our life to which we give in or one that is practiced with regularity. We can diligently begin to uproot it just as we might pull a weed that invades a beautiful garden.

Attention to the most menial duties with love and submission will bring gradual strength to achieve higher degrees of conformity to His will. Simple practices can form good habits of obedience. More steadfastness is involved in these little acts than what we think. Because of their reoccurrence, they require a strict watchfulness against any thought, word, or act that seeks our will and not God's. Knowing that Christ died for us, how can we do anything less?

July 2

> That is why we never give up. Though our bodies
> are dying, our spirits are being renewed every day.
>
> —2 Corinthians 4:16, NLT

There are days I look in the mirror and stare at the face looking back. How? When did this happen? I know aging develops wrinkles and sagging skin, but so many, so much, so fast?

I feel as though I am on a speeding train; I'm not the conductor, and I can't jump off.

Is it vanity? I have to believe it plays a role because, while I don't mind getting older, it would be nice to not *look* older.

I've used up all rationalization, and I am heading toward acceptance.

I cannot conquer the aging process, but I can rein in every obstacle that prohibits acceptance and appreciation. Every time I look in the mirror, I can thank Him for something. I still have all my teeth and no cavities!

I don't need a mirror to recognize that the one looking back is filled with gratitude beyond all that I can convey for this gift of life and the privilege of aging. My heart overflows with inexpressible joy of the blessings He has bestowed on me.

So I will celebrate my wrinkles and the sagging skin. Life and beauty are what we make them. Aging gracefully is all about enjoying it!

No matter our age, no matter what the mirror says, we are beautiful in the eyes of our Creator. Fashioned and designed by Him and for Him. We can sit back, relax, and enjoy the train ride!

Beautiful young people are accidents of nature, but beautiful old people are works of art.

—Eleanor Roosevelt

July 3

> Behold, God is my salvation, I will trust and not be
> afraid; for the Lord God is my strength and song,
> and He has become my salvation.
>
> —Isaiah 12:2, NASB

Father, I trust in You and will not be afraid. You are my strength and my song, and You give me victory over the lure of the world. You are my tower of refuge from the storm— my eternal rock.

You wait for me to come to You so You can show me Your love and compassion. You are faithful and gracious, and I rely on Your help.

Teach me, guiding my steps, and I will never be afraid. You are a God who does what is right, and You smooth out the path ahead of me (Isa. 26:7–9, NLT).

I show my trust in You by obeying Your laws. My heart's desire is to glorify Your name.

Thank you for Your promise of peace.

> What harm can happen to him who knows that
> God does everything, and who loves beforehand
> everything that God does?
>
> —Madame Swetchine

July 4

I am grateful for a human interest story in the nightly news. It helps dull a deep sense of sadness with the rest of what I am hearing. This morning, as I read Isaiah 1:2–4, I can't help but feel this scripture is also meant for us in America.

> Listen, O heavens! Pay attention, earth! This is what the Lord says:
> The children I raised and cared for have rebelled against Me. Even an ox knows its owner, and a donkey recognizes its master's care—but Israel doesn't know its master.
> My people don't recognize My care for them. Oh, what a sinful nation they are—loaded down with a burden of guilt. They are evil people, corrupt children who have rejected the Lord. They have despised the Holy One of Israel and turned their backs on Him.

We continue to pray for our nation and rely on this promise.

> Then if My people who are called by My name will humble themselves, and pray and seek My face, and turn from their wicked

ways, I will hear from heaven and will
forgive their sins and restore their land.

—2 Chronicles 7:14, NASB

July 5

Ponderings:

- "A man wrapped up in himself makes a very small bundle" (Benjamin Franklin).
- "Don't be afraid of an unknown future when you have a known God" (Corrie Ten Boom).
- "If you would advance in true holiness, you must aim steadily at perfection in little things" (Abbe Guillore).
- "Generosity is not giving me that which I need more than you do, but it is giving me that which you need more than I do" (Kahlil Gibran).
- "Faith is two empty hands held open to receive all of the Lord" (Anonymous).
- "There are two kinds of weakness; that which breaks and that which bends" (James Russell Lowell).
- "God loves us the way that we are, but He loves us too much to leave us that way" (Leighton Ford).

July 6

> The sound of Your thunder was in the whirlwind;
> The lightnings lit up the world; the earth trembled
> and shook.
>
> —Psalm 77:18, NASB

This morning we woke to an early thunder and lightning storm.

I grew up in Southern Colorado, and summer afternoon thunder storms were predictable. But in Southern California, which is facing one of the most severe droughts on record, it is more like an event!

Since my youth, lightning has frightened me; thunder has fascinated me.

As the rain pounds the sunroom windows, I browse through God's Word for references to thunder, the phenomenal *boom* heard overhead.

"Or do you have an arm like God, and can you *thunder* with a voice like His?" (Job 40:9, NASB; emphasis mine)

"The LORD also *thundered* in the heavens" (Ps. 18:13, NASB; emphasis mine).

"And there were flashes of lightning and sounds and peals of *thunder*" (Rev. 16:18, NASB; emphasis mine).

The greatness of God is displayed in nature as thunder rumbles and lighting streaks across the sky.

What a mighty God we serve!

July 7

Then Jesus told this story to some who had great confidence in their own righteousness and scorned everyone else:

Two men went to the Temple to pray. One was a Pharisee, and the other was a despised tax collector.

The Pharisee stood by himself and prayed this prayer: "I thank you, God, that I am not a sinner like everyone else. For I don't cheat, I don't sin, and I don't commit adultery. I'm certainly not like that tax collector! I fast twice a week, and I give You a tenth of my income."

But the tax collector stood at a distance and dared not even lift his eyes to heaven as he prayed. Instead, he beat his chest in sorrow, saying, "O God, be merciful to me, for I am a sinner."

I tell you, this sinner, not the Pharisee, returned home justified before God.

For those who exalt themselves will be humbled, and those who humble themselves will be exalted (Luke 18:9–14, NLT).

For the Word of God is alive and powerful. It is
sharper than the sharpest two-edged sword, cutting

between soul and spirit, between joint and marrow.
It exposes our innermost thoughts and desires.

—Hebrews 4:12, NLT

July 8

Heavenly Father, when the desire to be in Your presence is awakened in my soul, draw me near.

I need You!

I come to You and ask what You would have me to do. I believe You are ready to hear me when I pray. But I don't always know how to pray. I flounder, looking for words.

I know I am not worthy, but I love You with all my heart.

I am Your child, and I am inadequate. But by Your grace I am allowed to come to You.

Give me the realization of how much You love me! Teach me and help me. Then I will say with Paul, "Thanks be to God for His unspeakable gift!"

Love is the life of faith; obedience, the life of love.
Yea, rather, Christ Himself is the life of the soul.

—Edward B. Pusey

July 9

> You will show me the way of life, granting me the
> joy of Your presence and the pleasures of living
> with You forever.
>
> —Psalm 16:11, NLT

She came alongside but moved quickly down the beach. I felt like the tortoise; she the hare. It wasn't a competition, and she didn't offer a challenge, but still…

I tried to equal the number of steps she took, but she continued to increase the distance between us. It wasn't long and she was nearly out of sight. I accepted that I couldn't keep up and reluctantly resumed my regular pace.

As I continued my valuable walk, my attention turned to the sounds of the ocean. The thunderous waves slapped as they approached and slipped quietly onto the sand. A dozen pelicans glided single-file, skimming along the peak of a wave. Terns did a headlong dive into the water capturing their prey. Sanderlings, godwits, and plovers jabbed the wet sand looking for dinner. Grebes and cormorants submerged in and out of the shimmering water.

Yes, my slower pace afforded me time to savor the delicious sights and sounds of God's wondrous creation.

Lord, I don't want to hurry through life, to see how fast I can go, or to make it my goal to keep up with others. Slow me down that I may drink in all the wonder of You, not just in Your marvelous creation, but that I might commune with You, knowing that You delight in my companionship. Come alongside and walk with me.

July 10

> Have this attitude in yourselves which was
> also in Christ Jesus, who, although He existed
> in the form of God, did not regard equality
> with God a thing to be grasped, but emptied
> Himself, taking the form of a bond-servant,
> *and* being made in the likeness of men.
>
> —Philippians 2:5, NASB

There is a story that Abraham Lincoln went down to the slave block to buy back a slave girl. As she looked at the white man bidding on her, she figured he was another white man, going to buy her and then abuse her. He won the bid, and as he was walking away with his property, he said, "Young lady, you are free."

She said, "What does that mean?"

"It means you are free."

"Does that mean," she said, "that I can say whatever I want to say?"

Lincoln said, "Yes, my dear, you can say whatever you want to say."

"Does that mean," she said, "That I can be whatever I want to be?"

Lincoln said, "Yes, you can be whatever you want to be."

"Does that mean I can go wherever I want to go?"

He said, "Yes, you can go wherever you want to go."

And the girl, with tears streaming down her face, said, "Then I will go with you."

> God does not love us because we are valuable.
> We are valuable because God loves us.
>
> —Fulton J. Sheen

July 11

> You will keep in perfect peace all who trust in You,
> all whose thoughts are fixed on You!
>
> —Isaiah 26:3, NLT

I want to be strong, to meet my problems with peace. But sometimes when I am determined to do so, something arises that leaves me unable to cope.

And sometimes I am just sad. I believe You understand that, Lord, for there were times Your heart was sad.

Sad doesn't mean that I feel hopeless or helpless—just sad.

Maybe that's not such a bad thing. When I am sad for someone or sad about a situation, I know it is because I care.

I need once again to learn the lesson of perfect peace. I can do nothing on my own, and so I must discipline my mind to stay fixed on You.

I feel Your loving arms of comfort, recognizing my sad heart, for those I love who are struggling. I come before Your throne and wordlessly lay all this before You. I know it is here that You grant me peace.

He's the God of peace. If we steadfastly keep our thoughts fixed on Him and trust in Him for all things, we will experience perfect peace.

July 12

Wherever I may be, whatever I am doing, in my work, in all my undertakings, I ask that You be with me.

Then I will do everything as unto You, knowing that Your eye upon me will be the motive for my acts and words. I will do nothing that I would not have You see or say anything that I would not have You hear.

Proverbs 16:9 reminds me that I can make my plans, but You determine my steps.

Psalm 37:23 promises me that You direct my way and delight in every detail of my life.

I praise You, Lord, my God, my Savior! For each day You carry me in Your arms.

I wait quietly before You, for my victory comes from You. I will depend totally on You.

> The least look, the faintest expression, the casual act, may tell more of the secret power of Jesus in the soul than world-famed acts of self-devotion.
>
> —T. T. Carter

July 13

Child, watch out for people who cause divisions and upset your faith by teaching things that are contrary to what you have been taught. I tell you, stay away from them! Such people are not serving Me; they are serving their own personal interests. By smooth talk and glowing words they deceive innocent people.

When you obey Me, I am pleased. I want you to be wise in doing what is right and stay innocent of any wrong. My peace will crush Satan under your feet, and you will close your ears to false teaching. My grace is with you (Rom. 16:17–20, NLT).

Father, it is by Your grace that I can recognize those who would try to deceive me. You hide me in the shadow of Your wings. You are my fortress and my Savior, my rock in whom I find protection. You are my shield, the power that saves me. My heart rejoices, and my body rests in safety.

No one can lure me away from You with their smooth talk. To You be all the honor and glory!

> The grass withers and the flowers fade,
> but the Word of our God stands forever.
>
> —Isaiah 40:8, NLT

July 14

> Set a guard O Lord over my mouth, keep watch
> over the door of my lips.
>
> —Psalm 141:3, NASB

On a sunny afternoon I sat in my beach chair watching a flock of seagulls that lined the water's edge. A young man, his wife, and young son came across the sand. The father picked up a rock and threw it at an unsuspecting seagull standing in the water. The gull went down instantly, flapping and struggling. The woman looked shocked while the man laughed nervously, glancing around to see if anyone was watching. He took the little boy's hand, and the family moved down the beach.

The gull was helpless and unable to move. I don't believe this man really meant to hurt the bird. I think he threw the rock to show his son how the gull would fly if startled. But his thoughtless action caused pain and injury.

Gossip is like that. We throw stones and hurt people. We may not mean to do harm, but our words can leave someone helpless and hurt.

When I was a young mother, an acquaintance of mine became the talk of the town. I joined in the gossip, condemning her lifestyle. Words cannot describe the devastation I felt when I learned that she had taken her own life. I was ashamed of the role I had played in judging her instead of reaching out to help her.

Some try to justify gossip by stating that they are just being truthful and honest. But the Apostle Paul admonishes us, "Do not let any unwholesome talk come out of your mouths, but only what is helpful for building others up according to their needs, that it may benefit those who listen."

Consider this: stones can be used as weapons or as building blocks. How will you use the "stones" of your words?

May every word that comes from my mouth be pleasing to You, O Lord.

July 15

In Joshua 2 we read how God used the harlot, Rahab.

Joshua had sent two men as spies to check out Jericho. He believed the city to be heavily fortified, and he planned to conquer it. The men lodged at Rahab's house of prostitution.

Jericho was expecting an imminent attack from the Israelites, and when the king learned where the spies were hiding, he ordered Rahab to send them out. Instead she hid them up on the roof with stalks of flax and denied she knew them or where they might be.

That was a risky move. But she had to make a choice. If found out, she would die.

When it was safe to leave, she told the men, "I have dealt kindly with you. When you invade Jericho, please spare me and my family."

They said, "When we come into your land, tie this scarlet cord into the window and stay inside. No harm will come to you or your family."

God can work through someone like Rahab to accomplish His will. While we might reject her, God used her no matter what her profession. Could our faith withstand the pressure she was under? Would our split-minute decision be God's will? She put her life on the line.

It is wise to be careful when we judge someone. We never know if the person we reject may be God's instrument.

July 16

> Now the gates of Jericho were tightly shut because the people were afraid of the Israelites. No one was allowed to go out or in.
>
> —Joshua 6:1, NLT

Yesterday we read of two men who were sent by Joshua to check out Jericho. In Joshua 6 we follow the events of conquering the city.

You probably know the song "Joshua Fought the Battle at Jericho."

God told Joshua that He would deliver this heavily fortified city into his hands. In some places the walls around it were twenty-five feet high and twenty feet thick. Guards were posted on top of the walls and could see for miles. News that the Israelites had crossed the Jordan River was of grave concern, and the guards were increased to warn of any attack. The people remained within the walls.

Joshua's instructions from God were to march around the city once a day for six days. Seven priests walked ahead of the Ark, each carrying a ram's horn. They were told not to shout or let their voice be heard until the day Joshua would tell them to do so.

On the seventh day they marched around the city seven times with the trumpets blowing. After the seventh round, Joshua yelled, "Shout! For the LORD has given you the town!" (Josh. 6:16). They shouted, and the trumpets blew. The walls fell down, and the Israelites invaded the city. Everything was destroyed except Rahab and her family, who came to live with the Israelites.

Who would ever think that such a mighty fortress could crumble at the sounds of trumpets and shouting? It was brought about by obeying God's instructions.

There is no wall God can't bring down for us. Nothing is too great or too minor for God. Victory can be ours.

We must stay in His Word, follow His instructions, rely on His promises, and watch "the walls come tumbling down"!

July 17

Father, I am confident that You hear me whenever I ask for anything that pleases You. And so I humbly ask.

I pray that my love for You increases.

I pray that Your presence consumes me and all else dims in comparison to You.

I pray that my time be expanded so that I might find more of my day in solitude with You.

I pray that no thought or word be offensive to You but all I say and do pleases You, my God.

I pray that I respond to others with kindness, considering their needs greater than mine.

I pray that I live in the present and trust only You for tomorrow.

I pray for a thankful heart for all You have given me, even those testings and trials that are unfavorable.

I pray for patience.

I pray that I will cultivate silence that I might hear You.

I offer all that I have, all that I am. May You hear me and be pleased.

July 18

My sister and I were at a membership-only warehouse club when the doors opened that morning. Kevin, her young husband, was in the end of his life stage, and his sister was with him while we were gone. We moved quickly through the isles, checking items off the list.

The cart was pretty full when we got to checkout. Judy quickly unloaded the items onto the counter. She was almost finished when the clerk said, "This register is closing, would you please move over one?" Most of us would lose patience with that. Why didn't she say that before we had the cart almost empty?

But that day was particularly trying for Judy. She had bottled up her fears and emotions to make the trip to the store, knowing that it had to be done. But it would take little to break open the bottle.

Her face was flooded with emotion as she tried to suppress the outburst that was lying close to the surface. She grabbed items, throwing them back in the cart, proceeded to the next counter, and roughly unloaded them. Her anger was evident.

I wanted to explain her reaction to the clerk, who patiently smiled and checked us out rapidly. *She can't know what Judy is going through*, I thought.

That was a telling day for me. I want to view everyone I meet as someone who needs understanding no matter their reaction to things or maybe because of their reaction. I can't know what they are going through, but there are many wounded and fearful souls in our midst. I want to be a stepping stone and not a stumbling block. I will try to always remember that whomever I come in contact with, I am a living, breathing expression of Christ. I am made in His image, and I will live as such.

Every man has his secret sorrows which the world
knows not; and often times we call a man cold
when he is only sad.

—Henry Wadsworth Longfellow

July 19

Wait on the Lord; Be of good courage, and He
shall strengthen your heart; wait, I say, on the
Lord!

—Psalm 27:14, NKJV

The whole duty and blessedness of waiting on God has its root in this: that He is such a blessed Being, full to over-flowing, of goodness and power and life and joy, that we, however wretched, cannot for any time come into contact with Him, without life and power secretly, silently, beginning to enter into us and blessing us.

God is Love! God's love is just His delight to impart Himself and His blessedness to His children. Come, and however feeble you feel, just wait in His presence. As a feeble invalid is brought out into the sunshine to let its warmth go through him, come with all that is dark and cold in you into the sunshine of God's holy, omnipotent love, and sit and wait there, with the one thought: "Here I am in the sunshine of His love."

As the sun does its work in the weak who seeks its rays, God will do His work in you.[15]

July 20

Child, today you will never be out of My sight. I will be beside you, ahead of you, and behind you. I know when you sit down and when you get up. I even know what you will say before you say it.

My thoughts of you are so many you can't count them. They are more than the grains of sand on the beach. I have made you who you are, and I know every bone in your body. You are wonderfully made, just as I planned. You are Mine, and I love you. Please think of Me today.

> Made for Thyself, O God!
> Made for Thy love, Thy service, Thy delight!
> Made to show forth Thy wisdom, grace and might.
> Made for Thy praise, whom veiled archangels laud.
> O strange and glorious thought, that we may be a
>   joy to Thee! (F. R. Havergal)

July 21

Increase my faith, O Lord. So often it is weak.

Let my roots grow down into You, and I will draw nourishment from You. I want to grow in my relationship with You and become strong and vigorous in the truth.

After Jesus left the girl's home, two blind men followed along behind Him, shouting, "Son of David, have mercy on us!"

They went right into the house where He was staying, and Jesus asked them, "Do you believe I can make you see?"

"Yes, Lord," they told Him. "We do."

Then He touched their eyes and said, "Because of your faith, it will happen." Then their eyes were opened, and they could see! (Matt. 9:27–30, NLT)

Jesus, I believe You can do all things. The faith You have given me will grow stronger as I stand firmly in that faith and upon Your promises.

I will be courageous and strong in the truth because You strengthen me.

July 22

I will see you again.

—John 16:22, NLT

Child, don't let your hearts be troubled. Trust in God, and trust also in MeThere is more than enough room in My Father's home. If this were not so, would I have told you that I am going to prepare a place for you? When everything is ready, I will come and get you so that you will always be with Me where I am. And you know the way to where I am going (John 14:1–4).

If you let go of the worldly values that distract you, I will fill your thoughts with the valuable promise of heaven. The security of My promise relies on the measure of trust you have in Me. Don't waste your time on frivolous pastimes, those that count for nothing. Your life is to be hidden with Me in God. Yes, hidden—concealed and safe—as you look with expectation for My return.

When I come back again and am revealed to the whole world, you will share in My glory as I have promised (Col. 3:4, NLT).

> Commit yourself wholeheartedly
> to these words of Mine.
>
> —Deuteronomy 11:18, NLT

July 23

> I look up to the mountains.
>
> —Psalm 121:1, NLT

I look up!
I lift up my eyes to the mountains.
I know my help comes from You,
Creator of heaven and earth.
I know You will not allow me to fall nor my foot to slip.
You are my keeper, and I trust in You.
I look up!
I know You protect me from all evil.
You keep my soul,
And guard my comings and goings,
Today and forever.
I look up!

July 24

To really depend on God, we have to come to the end of ourselves. The discipline of disappointment often brings blessing into our lives. God uses both blessings and heartaches to reveal His love and grace and to communicate His messages to us.

Sometimes it takes seemingly insurmountable trouble and even pain to make us stop and listen to what God wants to reveal to us. If we don't listen to His voice and readily obey Him we lose our way.

And have you forgotten the encouraging words God spoke to you as His children? He said, "My child, don't make light of the Lord's discipline, and don't give up when He corrects you. For the Lord disciplines those He loves, and He punishes each one He accepts as His child" (Heb. 12:5–6, NLT).

> He will not spare discomfort or pain if in the end
> He can use the circumstance to make us more like
> Christ.
>
> —T. H. Epp

July 25

> Then Joshua told the people, "Purify yourselves,
> for tomorrow the Lord will do great wonders
> among you."
>
> —Joshua 3:5, NLT

We know that God parted the Red Sea, and the Israelites escaped from the Egyptian army. It was such a huge demonstration of His power that we might overlook the miracle of parting the Jordan River so that His people could enter Canaan, the Promised Land.

We read about it in Joshua 3.

It was spring, and the river was overflowing its banks. They had camped for three days when they were commanded to cross. God had promised Joshua that it was the day He would exalt him in the sight of the Israelites. Then His people would know that just as He had been with Moses, so "I will be with you."

Those who crossed the Red Sea were largely another generation. The Israelites had wandered for forty years before arriving here. And now at the Jordan River, the people revered Joshua and were ready to face what lie ahead with the man God had chosen to replace Moses. That day the waters of the Jordan rose in one heap, and they crossed the dry riverbed. It was a mighty display of God's power.

We must marvel at seeing God's plan for His people. They were complaining and ungrateful much of the time. "Why did we leave Egypt? This is too difficult! We will die before we even see the Promised Land!"

Stubborn and rebelling, they were pulled and pushed on their journey. God loved them and would see His promise fulfilled in spite of their stubbornness.

How many times has He parted the waters for us? Did we see it as a miracle?

July 26

Child, you have accepted Me as your Savior and therefore have been raised to new life with Me. This is difficult for you to grasp, I know. But you will thrive in this new life because I live in you!

Now you must put to death the sinful, earthly things lurking within you. Have nothing to do with sexual immorality, impurity, lust, and evil desires. Don't be greedy, for a greedy person is an idolater, worshipping the things of this world.

Before you found this new life, you did things that were part of this world. But now is the time to get rid of anger, rage, malicious behavior, slander, and dirty language.

Don't lie to each other, for you have stripped off your old sinful nature and all its wicked deeds. Put on your new nature and be renewed as you learn to know Me and become like Me (Col. 3:5–10, NLT).

In this new life, it doesn't matter who you are or what you have done. I am all that matters.

> Heaven and earth will disappear, but My words
> will never disappear.
>
> —Matthew 24:35, NLT

July 27

> All praise to God, the Father of our Lord Jesus
> Christ. God is our merciful Father and the source
> of all comfort. He comforts us in all our troubles
> so that we can comfort others. When they are
> troubled, we will be able to give them the same
> comfort God has given us.
>
> —2 Corinthians 1:1–4, NLT

Larry and I walked through the doors of the Polster Breast Care Center on a warm July morning. My yearly mammogram had shown an abnormality, and I was scheduled for an ultrasound guided biopsy.

I checked in, and we went to the waiting room. There were a couple of husbands flipping nervously through magazines.

My name was called, and I followed her to the changing room. I slipped into the pink gown she had given me and was directed to a lovely lounge where I waited to be called.

Minutes later, I am joined by another woman. I interrupt the momentary silence and ask, "Is this your first visit?" The technician is already at the door. "Patricia?" My fellow patient replies, "No, I'm a survivor." Our faces break into smiles. and we give the thumbs-up as I walk out.

"I'm a survivor!" Imagine if badges with those words were given to all those who have survived abuse, addiction, illness, grief. Just the word *survived* gives encouragement to those facing the unknown, just as I was that day.

When God comforts us, it doesn't mean that He relieves us of our troubles. Comforted can also mean receiving strength and encouragement when dealing with the battle. Experiencing God's comfort can enable us to comfort those who face the same challenges.

Days later I learned the lump was benign. As I thanked God for the result, I also thanked Him for giving me an appreciation of the word *survivor!*

July 28

Heavenly Father, I was once estranged from You.

I turned my back on You, following my own stubborn will. But You have been patient with me. You could not abandon me, for You are merciful. And in Your mercy, You have shown compassion. My sins separated me from You, but You have poured Your saving grace over me, drawing me back to You.

Now all glory to You, O God, who is able to keep me from falling away, and with great joy will bring me into Your glorious presence without a single fault.

All glory to You who alone are God.

All glory, majesty, power, and authority are Yours before all time, and in the present, and beyond all time! Amen (Jude 1:24–25, NLT).

July 29

He had been with Jesus throughout His earthly ministry. He was in the room when the risen Christ appeared to His disciples. He is a credible witness. Here is Peter's firsthand eyewitness account:

> Therefore, I will always remind you about these things—even though you already know them and are standing firm in the truth you have been taught. And it is only right that I should keep on reminding you as long as I live. For our Lord Jesus Christ has shown me that I must soon leave this earthly life, so I will work hard to make sure you always remember these things after I am gone.
>
> For we were not making up clever stories when we told you about the powerful coming of our Lord Jesus Christ. We saw His majestic splendor with our own eyes when He received honor and glory from God the Father. The voice from the majestic glory of God said to Him, "This is my dearly loved Son, who brings Me great joy." We ourselves heard

that voice from heaven when we were with Him on the holy mountain.

Because of that experience, we have even greater confidence in the message proclaimed by the prophets. You must pay close attention to what they wrote, for their words are like a lamp shining in a dark place—until the day dawns, and Christ the morning star shines in your hearts.

Above all, you must realize that no prophecy in Scripture ever came from the prophet's own understanding, or from human initiative. No, those prophets were moved by the Holy Spirit, and they spoke from God. (2 Pet. 1:12–21, NLT)

July 30

Lord, help me surrender to You those things with which I wrestle, the circumstances that trouble me.

There are loved ones who concern me. When I let go and release them to You, it doesn't mean that that I am giving up. Rather, I willingly give them over to You and trust in You for the outcome. Only then am I filled with the peace You promise.

When I surrender all to You, O Lord, I feel the serenity of Your peace. My inadequacy becomes confidence; my doubt becomes hope.

Today's challenges lie ahead, but we can meet them with Him who gives us hope and peace.

Child, Peace I leave with you, My peace I give to you; not as the world gives do I give to you. Let not your heart be troubled, neither let it be afraid (John 14:27, NKJV).

July 31

John gives us these words of caution:

> Do not love this world nor the things it offers you, for when you love the world, you do not have the love of the Father in you.
>
> For the world offers only a craving for physical pleasure, a craving for everything we see, and pride in our achievements and possessions. These are not from the Father, but are from this world. (1 John 2:15–16, NLT)

God, glorious Father of my Lord Jesus Christ, I heed these words. Give me wisdom and insight that I might grow in knowledge of You. I resist being lured by the cravings of the world.

Flood my heart with light so I can understand the confident hope You have given me.

I pray that I will understand the incredible greatness of Your power—the same mighty power that raised Christ from the dead and seated Him at Your right hand in the heavenly realm. This same power works in me to stand firm against the temptations this world offers.

You are far above any ruler or authority or power or leader or anything else, not only in this world, but in the world to come. I rely on Your grace (Eph. 1:16–21, NLT).

August 1

> Well done, good and faithful servant.
>
> —Matthew 25:21, NIV

Jesus was sitting on the Mount of Olives, and His disciples came to Him, privately asking Him what will be the sign of His coming again. He told them the day and hour is known only to God. But He warns that we must always be prepared.

He told them a parable about a man going on a journey who called his servants and entrusted his wealth to them, each according to his ability. He gave one five bags of gold, another two, and another one.

The man who had received five bags of gold immediately put his money to work and gained five bags more.

The one with two bags of gold gained two more. But the man who had received one bag went off, dug a hole in the ground, and hid his master's money.

When their master returned, he settled accounts with them. The man who had received five bags of gold showed him that he had made five more.

"Well done, good and faithful servant!" he said. "You have been faithful with a few things; I will put you in charge of many things. Come and share your master's happiness!"

The man with two bags of gold showed him that he had doubled it. The master said, "Well done, good and faithful servant!" You have been faithful with a few things; I will put you in charge of many things. Come and share your master's happiness!"

The man who had received one bag of gold came, and handed it to him. "Master, I know that you are a hard man, and I was afraid I would disappoint you, so I hid your gold in the ground."

His master replied, "You wicked, lazy servant! You were afraid? Well then, you should have put my money the bank. At least I would have received interest on it.

"Take the gold from him and give it to the one who has ten bags. For whoever has will be given more, and they will have an abundance. Whoever does not have, even what they have will be taken from them" (Matt. 25:14–28, NIV).

Jesus doesn't sugarcoat how we are to be prepared when He returns. We may not make headlines about the good use of our resources. But God knows. Our time, abilities, and money aren't ours. We must use the gifts He has entrusted to us. I think of the years I have wasted going about the things I felt important, ignoring His calling to use the gifts He has given me.

All things come from Him, and when we give back, it is our duty to do so. Then upon His return, He will call us to Himself, and we too shall hear the words, "Well done, good and faithful servant! You have been faithful with a few things; I will put you in charge of many things. Come and share your master's happiness!"

August 2

> Teach us to realize the brevity of life,
> so that we may grow in wisdom.
>
> —Psalm 90:12, NLT

Heavenly Father, life is brief.

This body will return to dust.

Please help me to number my days.

I want to use my time for eternal good, not earthly satisfaction.

I want to use it wisely, and for Your glory, that Your will might be fulfilled in my life.

A wise person thinks a lot about death, while a fool thinks only about having a good time (Eccles. 7:4, NLT).

Lord, remind me how brief my time on earth will be. Remind me that my days are numbered—how fleeting my life is.

> Our days on earth are as a shadow.
>
> —Job 8:9, NASB

August 3

Tax collectors and other notorious sinners often came to listen to Jesus teach. This made the Pharisees and teachers of religious law complain that He was associating with such sinful people—even eating with them! So Jesus told them this story:

> If a man has a hundred sheep and one of them gets lost, what will he do? Won't he leave the ninety-nine others in the wilderness and go to search for the one that is lost until he finds it?
>
> And when he has found it, he will joyfully carry it home on his shoulders. When he arrives, he will call

together his friends and neighbors, saying, 'Rejoice with me because I have found my lost sheep.

In the same way, there is more joy in heaven over one lost sinner who repents and returns to God than over ninety-nine others who are righteous and haven't strayed away! (Luke 15:1–7, NLT)

Jesus came to save all mankind. Whoever we meet today, Jesus's words can make a difference if we see them as one for whom for He died.

> When I discovered Your words, I devoured them.
> They are my joy and my heart's delight.
>
> —Jeremiah 15:16, NLT

August 4

> Blessed be His glorious name forever;
> may He fill all the earth with His glory.
> Amen and amen.
>
> —Psalm 72:19, NLT

Lord, if there is someone You want to bring to me today, someone hurting, needing understanding and compassion, I am here.

Use me. I want to yield myself completely to You.

I open my hands, Lord.

Take what you want and give me what You want me to have.

I meet this day with expectation. It will be of Your making, not mine.

I humbly submit to Your desire, knowing that I will be blessed when I obey You.

Anything I do, when done in Your name, will bring You the honor and the glory.

Thank You for going ahead of me, surrounding me with Your grace that I will live according to all You ask of me.

August 5

> But blessed are those who trust in the Lord and
> have made the Lord their hope and confidence.
>
> —Jeremiah 17:7, NLT

I long for a tranquil spirit. If I begin my day in quiet communion with God, I find those circumstances that invade my life don't take me captive. My dependence upon Him is my only source of rising above the turmoil.

Thomas C. Upham writes, "Divine tranquility grows from the life of God in the soul, which is the same as the life of pure love. Why should a soul be otherwise than tranquil, which seeks for nothing but what comes in the prudence of God, and which, forgetful of self, has nothing to do but love? It has an innate conviction, strong as the everlasting foundations, that, if there is a God above us, all is well, all must be well."

> Thus will I live and walk from day to day,
> contented, trustful, satisfied, and still.
> What life so shielded, or what life so free,
> as that within the center of Thy will! (Jane Woodfall)

August 6

Lord, I know it is not within my power to map out my life, to decide its course.

You direct my steps and hold my hand.

You guide me with Your counsel, leading me to a glorious destiny (Ps. 73:23–24, NLT).

I will not be afraid or discouraged, for You will personally go ahead of me.

You will neither fail me nor abandon me (Deut. 1:8, NLT).

I am Yours.

I come boldly and confidently before Your throne, O gracious God, for You promise me mercy and the grace to help me when I need it most.

Righteousness and justice are the foundation of Your throne.

Your light shines on me, and joy floods my heart.

I rejoice in You, O mighty God, and praise Your holy name!

August 7

> Work willingly at whatever you do, as though you
> were working for the Lord rather than for people.
>
> —Colossians 3:23, NLT

Lord, I love you, and I offer You the whole use of my day. From when I open my eyes to the light of the morning to when I close them at night,

I will spend my time in active service for You or in silent prayer, according to Your pleasure.

I won't select the most agreeable task but whatever You may want it to be. I will be as a straw on the current of a river, flowing and moving in the direction to which You want to take me.

I serve You with no thought of reward or recognition from anyone, working only for You that in all my actions You may be glorified.

Have you ever realized that you can give things to God that are of value to Him? Or are you just sitting around daydreaming about the greatness of His redemption, while neglecting all the things you could be doing for Him? I'm not referring to works which could be regarded as divine and miraculous, but ordinary, simple human things—things which would be evidence to God that you are totally surrendered to Him. (Oswald Chambers)

August 8

Do not be conformed to this world, but be
transformed by the renewing of your mind, that
you may prove what *is* that good and acceptable
and perfect will of God.

—Romans 12:2, NKJV

Lord, today help me treat with kindness everyone I meet.

Help me to be patient when I am feeling impatient.

Help me recognize that beneath someone's rudeness or unkind words lays hurt or sorrow about which I know nothing.

Help me offer a smile and kind word when I may not feel like it.

Help me to consider it a privilege to listen to another's problems when I feel I have enough of my own.

Help me not to judge anyone whom I deem as different.

Help me not to complain but to offer all physical ailments and difficulties to You.

Help me to love everyone as I love myself and do to them what I would have others do to me.

And when today is done, I will be thankful for Your help and for the peace it has brought as I live to please You above all else.

August 9

> Anyone who is thirsty may come to Me. Anyone who believes in Me may come to drink. For the scriptures declare, "Rivers of living water will flow from his heart."
>
> —John 7:37–38, NLT

Lord, I think of Your tender love for the Samaritan woman when she came to the well. You asked if she would give You a drink from her well. She questioned why a Jew would ask a Samaritan for anything. Your response delights my heart!

"If you only knew the gift God has for you, and who you are speaking to, you would ask Me, and I would give you living water" (John 4:10, NLT).

"Anyone who drinks this water will soon become thirsty again. But those who drink the water I give will never be thirsty again. It becomes a fresh, bubbling spring within them, giving them eternal life" (John 4:13–14, NLT).

Yes, Lord Jesus, fill me with living water; quench my thirst!

Pour over me; drench me in the water of eternal life that I may never thirst again.

God often chooses the greatest sinners to receive His greatest graces.

August 10

Jesus, You are the eternal Word. You existed in the beginning with God. He created everything through You, and nothing was created except through You.

You gave life to everything that was created, and Your life brought life to everyone.

Your light shines in the darkness, and the darkness can never extinguish it (John 1:1–5, NLT)

I know that nothing is hidden from You.

Darkness can blind me, and I can't see my way. I want to live in Your light—illuminated! Lit up! Then our intimate relationship can be seen by all.

Light my way, Lord Jesus; lead me, and I will never fear the darkness.

> See the goodness all around you,
> even if you have to squint to do so.
>
> —Dennis Keating

August 11

> So then, since Christ suffered physical pain, you
> must arm yourselves with the same attitude He
> had, and be ready to suffer too.
>
> —1 Peter 4:1, NLT

I sit in the guest bedroom reading Your Word. I hear the moan of pain from down the hall. Kevin is having a bad day. My fifty-five-year old brother-in-law has terminal cancer and is under hospice care.

Lord, I know You understand when I ask, "Why? Why suffering?" I seek answers, and returning to my reading, You answer me.

Child, I suffered physical pain. Scripture tells you that My face was so disfigured I hardly seemed human, and from My appearance one would scarcely know I was a man (Isa. 52:14, NLT).

I was beaten so you could be whole, whipped so You could be healed. It was in Gethsemane that I bowed My face to the ground praying, "Father, if You are willing, please take this cup of suffering away from Me. Yet I want Your will to be done, not Mine" (Luke 22:42, NLT).

Yes, I understand suffering and pain. Since I Myself have gone through testing, I am able to help those who are being tested. I am refining them, but not as silver is being refined. Rather I am refining them in the furnace of suffering (Isa. 48:10, NLT).

Experience My mighty power. I will raise you up all who know Me, and you will live with Me eternally, free from suffering and pain.

Kevin was always in pain. Early on in the process he asked his wife, "Did I tell you how I handle the pain?"

Judy said, "No."

He said, "Jesus Christ suffered more than I ever will suffer, and knowing that, I can deal with the pain."

Lord God, the *why* of suffering I may never know, but You will sustain those who do. Thank You for Your Word.

The Lord received Kevin four months later, December 11, 2014.

August 12

> Joyful in hope, patient in affliction,
> and faithful in prayer.
>
> —Romans 12:12, NIV

You are a shield around me; You are my glory, and You hold my head high.

I have cried to You with my voice, and You have answered me from Your holy mountain.

I have laid down, slept, and woke in safety.

You watch over me.

You sustain me.

I am not afraid. Even if ten thousand armies surround me, I will trust in You (Ps. 3:6, NLT).

I will praise You, Lord, with all my heart; I will tell of all the marvelous things You have done.

I am filled with joy because of You and will sing praises to Your name, O most high God (Ps. 9:1–2, NLT).

Rest your soul in His embrace. Let Him hug you.

August 13

Some days on my beach walk I come across a collection of seashells pocketed in a cluster lying on the sand. The conch, cone, clam, sand dollars, scallops, and others too numerous to mention are commonly found on this beach. Few of the shells in this collection are perfectly sculptured and intact. Most are sea-worn and disfigured. Some are but broken fragments of what once was.

God's handiwork from the sea is on display. I consider each one a unique miracle of His hand.

The Lord does whatever pleases Him throughout all heaven and earth and on the seas and in their depths. He causes the clouds to rise over the whole earth. He sends the lightning with the rain and releases the wind from His storehouses (Ps. 135:6–7, NLT).

And He drops the seashells on the beach. God grants us joy and pleasures from His mighty works in the heavens to the treasures on the sand. When we abide in Him and He in us, we are filled with wonder of all His ways.

We may be worn, or fragments of brokenness, or untarnished by life, yet we are each one His miracle—each one His awesome design, pocketed in a cluster here on earth.

Father, when we see the work of Your hands, Your majestic name fills the earth. Your glory is higher than the heavens. We will sing praises to You forever.

August 14

Be still and know that I am God!

—Psalm 46:10, NASB

The world today is noisy. Noise can be a distraction. When communicating with the Creator of the universe, the noise level must drop. Secret thoughts are best found in silence.

God is our Father, and He speaks in silence. At Christ's baptism, and later when Christ revealed Himself on the mountain of transformation, God spoke out loud to those present. Both instances are God's validation and approval of Christ's ministry.

Most of the time God speaks to us in silence. We have to stop what we are doing and concentrate on hearing and understanding His voice when He speaks.

He speaks to us most often in the silence of our minds. We learn to listen to His voice. He whispers but seldom roars. Many believers have had their prayer lives hampered by impatience—in not taking enough time to hear God's voice.

"After the fire came a gentle whisper" (1 Kings 19:33, NIV).

Elijah ran for his life from Jezebel, one of the most evil women who ever lived. She wanted to catch this evasive prophet of Jehovah and put his head on a stick.

Elijah, when he heard this threat, literally ran for his life, deep into the silence of the desert. At a certain point while resting, our God Jehovah spoke to him, the discouraged, bewildered, exhausted prophet.

Great moments of accomplishment in our spiritual life are often followed by the threat of great moments of failure, danger, or fear.

The angel came to Elijah, not in the traditional ways of God speaking to mankind through powerful vocal messages, or visual demonstrations of His power (wind, fire, water, etc.). The angel revealed the most important message of encouragement, power, peace, and protection to Elijah in a whisper!

Those of us who know Jesus Christ as our Savior must learn to listen![15]

August 15

Your Word continues to nourish me each morning. Today I am rushed and depart from my usual structured Bible readings and search the scriptures that You have for me to read. I am not disappointed!

You said, "Let there be light in the darkness," and You have made the light shine in my heart so that I can know Your glory that is seen in the face of Jesus (2 Cor. 4:6, NLT).

He became a human being and lived here on earth, full of unfailing love and faithfulness. I want to follow Your example.

No one has ever seen You but Jesus, who is Himself God. He is near to my heart and has revealed You to me (John 1:18, NLT).

I thirst for You, the Living God. When can I stand before You? (Ps. 42:2, NLT)

I praise You that the Spirit works in me to make me more like You as I am changed into Your glorious image (2 Cor. 3:18, NLT).

Thank You for the gift of Your Word and for the Light that expels the darkness in me!

August 16

> Through suffering, our bodies continue to share in
> the death of Jesus so that the life of Jesus may also
> be seen in our bodies.
>
> —2 Corinthians 4:10, NLT

If we are faithful and humble, God will increase our faith by enabling us to obey more faithfully and will strengthen our sight by enabling us to do what we now see. As in our daily walk, where we come nearer toward heaven, He will open to us more of heaven.

And so the veil, which sin laid upon our sight, being taken away, "we all, with open face, beholding, as in a glass, the glory of the Lord."

Studying His countenance, watching His looks, seeking to have His gracious and compassionate look cast upon us in the midst of our frailties and infirmities may catch some faint reflections of its brightness and be changed into the image where we gaze, which we love, which in our weakness, we would long to copy and transfuse into ourselves; we too may be changed into the same image from glory to glory as by the Spirit of the Lord.[16]

August 17

> Follow God's example, therefore, as dearly loved
> children and walk in the way of love, just as Christ
> loved us and gave Himself up for us as a fragrant
> offering and sacrifice to God.
>
> —Ephesians 5:1–2, NLT

I am grateful that I have accepted You as my Lord and strive to follow You.

I want my roots to grow down deep into You and my life be built on You.

My heart overflows with thanksgiving as my faith grows stronger in the truth.

I want to imitate You in everything I do, to live a life filled with love following Your example.

You love me and offered Yourself as a sacrifice for me, a pleasing aroma to God.

Before I gave my life to You, I was full of darkness, but now I have light from You. I want to live in Your light, for it produces in me only what is good, and right, and true (Eph. 5:8–10, NLT).

Help me determine what pleases You, Lord Jesus.

> O rest of rests! O peace, serene, eternal!
> Thou ever livest, and Thou changest never,

And in the secret of Thy presence dwelleth
Fullness of joy, forever and forever. (Harriet Beecher
Stowe)

August 18

> Every good thing given and every perfect gift
> is from above, coming down from the Father
> of lights, with whom there is no variation or a
> shifting shadow.
>
> —James 1:17, NASB

Child, rest in Me, and I will reveal abundant peace. You will find true peace only when I am the center of your life.

I have made you for Myself; repose in Me. Your craving for peace is a natural yearning in your soul. I will fill it. Nothing less than Me can satisfy it.

I will dwell in you.

Father, I want to commune with You, not always with deliberate thoughts or words formed to be expressed at a certain time, but with feelings that fill my heart. Those times when feelings spill into words of praise and worship are the Holy Spirit working in me.

But even when I experience times of weariness and dryness, I will tell You.

Each moment, no matter what I am doing, grant that Your quiet and serene presence fill my soul and spirit. Quiet and serenity—Your good and perfect gifts!

You are the center of my life; nothing but You can satisfy the longing in my soul.

August 19

> And so I tell you, keep on asking,
> and you will receive what you ask for.
>
> —Luke 11:9, NLT

Jesus, I have prayed for so many years concerning my loved one. For periods of time I get disheartened. I'm not sure You are listening. Time passes, and I quit asking.

And then I read what You want me to know. I cling to this promise. You told the parable of a man going to a friend's house at midnight wanting to borrow three loaves of bread for he had a guest arrive very late and had nothing for him to eat.

But his friend tells him that "It's late, don't bother me, I can't help you." Then You assure us with this promise:

> "Though he won't do it for friendship's sake, if you
> keep knocking long enough, he will get up and give

you whatever you need because of your shameless persistence.

And so I tell you, keep on asking, and you will receive what you ask for. Keep on seeking, and you will find. Keep on knocking, and the door will be opened to you.

For everyone who asks, receives.

Everyone who seeks, finds.

And to everyone who knocks, the door will be opened.

You fathers—if your children ask for a fish, do you give them a snake instead? Or if they ask for an egg, do you give them a scorpion? Of course not! So if you sinful people know how to give good gifts to your children, how much more will your heavenly Father give the Holy Spirit to those who ask Him?" (Luke 11:5–13, NLT)

Lord, You aren't going to get rid of me! I am going to keep on asking!

> How sweet Your words taste to me:
>   they are sweeter than honey.
>
> —Psalm 119:103, NLT

August 20

> Let Me teach you, because I am humble and gentle
> at heart, and you will find rest for your souls.
>
> —Matthew 11:29, NLT

Let us seek the attitude of Jesus. Although He was God, He didn't think equality with His Father as something to be used to His own advantage; rather, He made Himself nothing by taking the very nature of a servant, being made in human likeness.

He didn't cease being God when He became a human being, but He set aside the right to His glory and power.

We see one example of His servant's heart in John 13:3–16 when He rose from the table, took the basin and towel, and began to wash the feet of the disciples. Walking in sandals on the dirt roads of Palestine made it imperative that feet be washed before a communal meal. People reclined at a low table, and guests could see each other's dirty feet. Usually a servant washed the feet of the guests, but there wasn't a servant at this supper. Did it occur to the disciples to wash each other's feet or at least the Master's?

Jesus was doing the work of the lowliest servant.

The timing was perfect because not long before this the disciples were disputing as to which of them was to be regarded as the greatest.

When He finished washing their feet, He told them, "I have given you an example that you should do as I have done to you."

Can we emulate this measure of servitude? Do we consider ourselves servants, or do we question, "Why do I have to do that?" In our home or workplace, are we willing to step up and serve by Christ's example? Do our actions exhibit a servant's heart for our children to follow?

Jesus says He will teach us gentleness and humility. We can read His Word and follow His example.

> Humility is not a one-time lesson that comes when you have lost everything. It is a daily reminder of how far we have come, yet still short of who we can be through His guidance.
>
> Blessed is the soul that can recognize that he isn't moving mountains, but God is for him.
>
> —Shannon L. Alder

August 21

I come to You, Lord, searching Your Word for what You would have me do when fear creeps in. I hate when that happens! I seek Your assurance.

Deuteronomy 31:6 tells me to be strong and courageous, not to be afraid and not to panic. You will personally go ahead of me. You will neither fail me nor abandon me.

Psalm 112:7–8 offers me hope. Because I trust in You, I won't fear bad news but confidently trust You to care for me. When I am confident and fearless, I can face anything triumphantly because You are with me.

And thank You for Your promise in Romans 16:20 that Your peace will soon crush Satan under my feet.

Lord, I pray that You, the source of hope, will fill me completely with joy and peace because I trust in You. Then I will overflow with confident hope through the power of the Holy Spirit (Rom. 15:13).

Oh, yes, I have prayed, Lord, and You answered me. Whatever lies ahead, I know You are with me.

Blessings can come disguised as not-so-good, difficult, and life-changing. We recognize the blessing only after we've made it through.

August 22

> Therefore, as *the* elect of God, holy and beloved,
> put on tender mercies, kindness, humility,
> meekness, longsuffering.
>
> —Colossians 3:12, NKJV

It seems far-fetched to think of ourselves as becoming holy. But that is our calling when we follow Christ. We throw away our past as we might throw away old clothing. And we put on new attractive garments, which array us in holiness.

Paul writes in 2 Corinthians that if we are in Christ, we are a new creature; the old things have passed away, and the new things have come. We are brand new! We have joined our lives to His. We are His elect; we are chosen. Jesus said that many are called, but few are chosen.

Father, I know I cannot become holy by trying. But as I leave behind my old life of sin and trust in You, I can change attitudes and habits that stifle my growth, preventing me from being holy. Change may be slow, but through the power of the Holy Spirit, I will live according to the way You would have me to live.

Then I will be pleasing in Your sight, holy and blameless on the day of Your return.

The very essence of Your words is truth.

—Psalm 119:160, NLT

August 23

Nothing will harm you.

—Luke 10:19, NIV

The little guy was about eighteen months old, with curly blond hair and wearing his long board shorts. Dad was trying to coax him down the sand to the ocean. He would dart forward a few steps, encouraging his son to chase him. But he would have nothing to do with it. He stood there crying and shaking his head. Finally, Dad lovingly scooped him up, kissed him, and headed to the water.

I didn't break my stride. I hoped I would see the outcome on my return, but they were gone.

Often we are like that little one. We don't want to do it and stand firmly planted, refusing to leave our comfort zone. The challenge ahead seems as wide and deep as the ocean that the youngster faced. I imagine the underlying factor is fear. But when stubbornness kicks in, our loving heavenly Father scoops us up and carries us. We are secure in His arms and ready to face the challenge.

Father God, no matter what this day holds for me, I will surrender to Your loving arms, knowing You will carry me through whatever would hinder me from relying on Your wisdom, love, and kindly care.

August 24

Lord, in Romans 13:10–12 You remind me that love does no wrong to others, so love fulfills the requirements of Your law.

And You tell me this is urgent.

Wake up. Salvation is near. The night is almost gone; the day of salvation will soon be here. So remove your dark deeds like dirty clothes and put on the shining armor of right living.

Because I belong to the day, I must live a decent life for all to see. You have brought me from darkness into light. That light is piercingly bright, and it illuminates the awful reality of sin. Because of the light, I recognize how debilitating sin is in my life.

I want to live in the light, shedding anything that blurs my vision of You. Evil desires distance me from You.

Your Word is the light that directs me; it shows me the way that leads to You. I will follow the Light!

August 25

> Trust in the Lord with all your heart.
>
> —Proverbs 3:5, NASB

I push open the massive, ornate door with ease, and step into the foyer. Its cool marble floor is pleasant to my bare feet. I take in the extravagant surroundings.

The soft light streaming in from the rafter-high stained glass windows floods the room. I stand motionless in awe of the incredible beauty.

I am in the Mansion of Trust!

The Lord has led me here. I could have resisted His call and gone the other direction, to where only a sparsely furnished shack waited for me. But He wants to lavish me with riches, and so I follow Him.

I look around. The numerous halls and rooms are furnished with blessings that are everywhere. Grace fills every corner. There is no room for fear, sorrow, or weariness. Joy, peace, and patience reside here.

His perfect peace sweeps through me; I feel His divine goodness, the beauty of His holiness. My serene spirit delights in being here with Him.

The only voice I hear echoes softly throughout, "Be still and know that I am God!"

I love it here! I don't want to leave. No matter what lies ahead, the Mansion of Trust is my home. I have settled in.

August 26

> For then the dust will return to the earth,
> and the spirit will return to God who gave it.
>
> —Ecclesiastes 12:7, NLT

We might look with envy at the beautiful, the rich, and powerful until we remember that our bodies will decay; we can't take our possessions with us, and the powerful will surrender with the last breath.

Solomon was the son of King David. He is known as the wisest man who ever lived. He strayed from God, but near the end of his life he wrote Ecclesiastes, reflecting on his life. He writes:

> God gives some people great wealth and honor and everything they could ever want, but then He doesn't give them the chance to enjoy these things. They die, and someone else, even a stranger, ends up enjoying their wealth! This is meaningless—a sickening tragedy. (Eccles. 6:2, NLT)

> In the few days of our meaningless lives, who knows how our days can best be spent? Our lives are like a shadow. Who can tell what will happen on this earth after we are gone? (Eccles. 6:12, NLT)

Enjoy what you have rather than desiring what you don't have. Just dreaming about nice things is meaningless—like chasing the wind.

Much of what he writes in Ecclesiastes seems negative. He ends with "Here now is my final conclusion; fear God and obey His commands, for this is everyone's duty" (Eccles. 12:13–14, NLT).

The certainty of death repudiates all our human achievements and reminds us that this life will end. The contentment we find in the success of this life is temporary, but life centered on God is eternal.

August 27

Lord, I show You my love by obeying Your commandments.

I want to live in such a way that I will not cause another to stumble or fall.

Whatever I do, I will do it all for Your glory.

Fill me with the knowledge of Your will. Give me spiritual wisdom and understanding so the way I live will honor You.

Whatever I do, may I be Your representative to the world.

Show me the right path, O Lord. Point me to the road You want me to follow. Show me Your ways, Lord, teach me Your paths. Guide me in Your truth and teach me, for You are God my Savior, and my hope is in You all day long (Ps. 25:4–5, niv).

How amazing are Your deeds, O Lord. We delight in You and ponder all Your ways. Even when we resist, You persist!

August 28

> Please take my life from me,
> for death is better to me than life.
>
> —Jonah 4:2, nlt

Depression is a human calamity. It has been called the common cold of mental disorders, and one source estimates that it disrupts the lives of thirty to forty million Americans.

Sometimes it strikes when hard times, grief, or sorrow invade our lives. I have experienced that.

But for some, depression is a lingering dark cloud that inhabits mind, body, and soul. They may function when things are going okay, and yet the depression lies in wait to gain control once again. It is a tenacious enemy, driven by a fierce need to conquer the spirit.

This enemy can destroy relationships, driving away loved ones and friends. It leads to job loss and often times addictions.

Some cases of depression may be caused by chemical imbalances, but one can live a fruitful life with prescribed medication.

Many great men in Old Testament times experienced bouts of depression. Among them are Abraham, Jonah, Job, Elisha, King Saul, and Jeremiah.

Many of us know someone who suffers with depression. I do. I pray faithfully that God will release him from the devastation of the disease.

I know that God saw him before he was born! Every day of his life is recorded in His book. Every moment was laid out before a single day had passed.

God's thoughts toward him are too numerous to count; they outnumber the grains of sand. (Ps. 139:17–18, NASB).

> Yes, we know that God loves them more than we do.
> The Lord is righteous in everything He does;
> He is filled with kindness.
> The Lord is close to all who call on Him in truth.
> He grants the desires of those who fear Him;
> He hears their cries for help and rescues them. (Ps. 145:17–19, NASB)

August 29

1 Thessalonians 5:12–22 tells me that I must honor those who are leaders in Your work, who work hard and give spiritual guidance I am to show them great respect and wholehearted love because of their work. I am to live peacefully with everyone.

And I am to warn those who are lazy.

Encourage those who are timid.

Take tender care of those who are weak.

Be patient with everyone.

I am not to pay back evil for evil but always try to do good to all people.

You tell me to always be joyful.

Never stop praying.

Be thankful in all circumstances, for this is Your will for me and all who belong to You.

I must never stifle the Holy Spirit.

I am not to scoff at prophecies but test everything that is said.

Hold on to what is good and stay away from every kind of evil.

This is quite a list, Lord. I know I will never achieve these in my lifetime. But I will continue to stay in Your Word and rely on Your power within me so that little by little I will follow Your example.

Through Your Word, O Lord, You guide me, giving me peace.

August 30

If I speak in the tongues of men or of angels, but do not have love, I am only a resounding gong or a clanging cymbal.

If I have the gift of prophecy and can fathom all mysteries and all knowledge, and if I have a faith that can move mountains, but do not have love, I am nothing. If I give all I possess to the poor and give over my body to hardship that I may boast, but do not have love, I gain nothing (1 Cor. 13:1–3).

Substituting *love* with *I* in verses 4–7, am I able to say with honesty:

I am patient.

I am kind.

I do not envy.

I do not boast.

I am not proud.

I do not dishonor others.

I am not self-seeking.

I am not easily angered.

I keep no record of wrongs.

I do not delight in evil but rejoice with the truth.

I always protect, always trust, always hope, and always persevere.

Lord, when I say this out loud, I am convicted of my lack of true love. I want to love as You love!

Fill me with Your Spirit so that love isn't something that I do, but love is who I am.

August 31

> Yes, my soul, find rest in God;
> my hope comes from Him.
>
> —Psalm 62:5, NIV

The past few weeks I have taken walks in the neighborhood with my sister and her closest companion, Rupert, a mixed breed. Most of the time he is on the leash, but there are areas along the way that my sister regularly releases him to explore. With discipline he has learned to stay close and responds to her voice commands.

When coming to an intersection, she says, "Sit." He plants himself, looking up at her, then across the street and back at her. He's thinking, *When?* When all is clear she says, "Go!" and Rupert charges across the street.

I chuckle to think of comparing my wait to that of Rupert's. But I find similarities.

The Lord is my closest companion and has disciplined me, teaching me to obey His commandments. He has given me free will and allowed me to make choices. But I have learned to stay close to Him and respond to His voice. And in the major trials and minor difficulties, I have learned to wait on Him, trusting Him.

I feel like I am sitting on the corner at the intersection, waiting and asking *when?* You bid me to sit and wait until You give the go-ahead. "Be still and know that I am God" (Ps. 46:10, NIV). I am impatient and want to dash forward.

I am here once again; my human nature in conflict with the Spirit. I am anxious. But only He knows when it is time. I will stay planted until He says, "Go!"

September 1

> I know whom I have believed, and am convinced
> that He is able to guard what I have entrusted to
> Him until that day.
>
> —2 Timothy 1:12, NIV

Paul had suffered for Christ's sake, proclaiming the gospel, and even though he was in prison when he wrote these words, he continued to trust his Savior.

Christ will return for us and take us with Him to the heavenly Kingdom to reign with Him forever. But in the meantime, we live in a challenging world. Following Jesus is not always easy. A scribe came to Him and said, "Teacher, I will follow You wherever You go." Jesus said to him, "The foxes have holes and the birds of the air have nests, but the Son of Man has nowhere to lay His head" (Matt. 8:20, NIV).

To what measure are we willing to follow Jesus? He says, "Not everyone who says to me, 'Lord, Lord,' will enter the kingdom of heaven, but only the one who does the will of My Father who is in heaven" (Matt. 7:21, NIV).

Our prisons may not be bars, but we can be captive to the lures of Satan, thus making a prison for ourselves. Jesus has saved us and called us to a holy life—not because of anything we have done, but because of His own purpose and grace. Are we willing to follow His will at any cost?

September 2

> For the Lord Himself will come down from
> heaven with a commanding shout, with the voice
> of the archangel, and with the trumpet call of God.
> First, the believers who have died will rise from
> their graves. Then, together with them, we who are
> still alive and remain on the earth will be caught
> up in the clouds to meet the Lord in the air. Then
> we will be with the Lord forever. Encourage each
> other with these words.
>
> —1 Thessalonians 4:16–18, NLT

And so it will be that Jesus Himself in all His majesty will descend, even as He had ascended from heaven. A shout will be given ordering the dead to rise. An archangel summoning all of God's elect with the sound of a trumpet will repeat the order.

When all the dead in Christ are raised and their bodies made glorious, those who are still alive will be caught up together with them in the clouds to meet our Lord God in the air. Yes, those of us who are in Christ, having been cleansed by the blood of the Lamb, will be caught up with our loved ones who have died and taken to our eternal glory to be forever with the Lord. What a glorious promise!

Although death has separated us from our loved ones, we will meet again. We and all God's people will be with Him forever more. I look with hope and anticipation to Your return, my Lord and my God.

> Heaven and earth will pass away,
> but My words will never pass away.
>
> —Matthew 24:35, NLT

September 3

> But we are citizens of heaven,
> where the Lord Jesus Christ lives.
>
> —Philippians 3:20, NLT

We are citizens of heaven! If we don't think about citizenship much, we may not value what this means. Because of it, we are vested with the rights, privileges, and duties of a citizen. Citizenship is vital, but it is easy to take it for granted. The first question might be to ask ourselves how important is our citizenship to us.

The times we have traveled out of the country and presented our passports at immigration, I have felt a sense of pride as an American citizen. It doesn't come from a feeling of superiority or haughtiness but one of gratitude.

And so it is for us who belong to God. We are only visitors here on earth for a brief time. We will arrive in heaven, where Jesus sits at the right hand of the Father, expecting our arrival. Our passport has been issued, and we will be given immediate access to heaven.

We have a priceless inheritance—an inheritance that is kept in heaven for us, pure and undefiled, beyond the reach of change and decay. Our weak mortal bodies will be changed into glorious bodies.

Anticipating our inheritance, let us dwell on heavenly things and not earthly things, for in His time, we will be with Him in our heavenly home, where we hold our citizenship.

September 4

I receive nothing unless You give it. As I become less, You become more.

You have come from heaven and reign over all. You were sent by the Father and spoke His words, for He gave You the Spirit without limit. He loves You and put everything in Your hands.

Because I believe in You, You give me eternal life. You died and rose from the dead. You are my God while I live and when I die.

Therefore, God elevated Him to the place of highest honor
and gave Him the name above all other names,
that at the name of Jesus every knee should bow,
in heaven and on earth and under the earth,
and every tongue declare that Jesus Christ is Lord,
to the glory of God the Father. (Phil. 2:9–11, NLT)

Live by every word that comes
from the mouth of the Lord.

—Deuteronomy 8:3, NLT

September 5

I brought my iPad with me this morning while doing my Bible study lesson. I was expecting an e-mail. Each time the ringtone notified me there was an e-mail, I looked at it.

After a few of them, none of which I was expecting, I thought, *What am I doing?* The interruptions were robbing me of precious time in God's Word. I felt I had been cheated, and it was my own fault. I had my priorities mixed up.

I thought of the times I have tried to visit with someone whose cell phone was the third party. Each time a call came through, they answered. Whether it is important or not to them, I don't like it. Here I was alone with God, and I was doing the same thing!

This was going to be a challenging day as it was. I had come into His presence seeking His strength and patience for what it might bring. I knew I couldn't be prepared without His help.

Deuteronomy 4:29 promises me, "If you seek the Lord your God, you will find Him if you seek Him with all your heart and with all your soul."

Well I certainly had not done that! I put the iPad back where it belongs. I need to be here! Everything else can wait; nothing is more important than being alone with Him.

September 6

I am blessed because I trust in You, my Lord and my God. I have made You my hope and confidence.

You thrill me, Lord, with all You have done for me! O Lord, what great works You do! And how deep are Your thoughts.

> The LORD is king! He is robed in majesty.
> Indeed, the LORD is robed in majesty and armed
> with strength.
> The world stands firm
> and cannot be shaken.

Your throne, O Lord, has stood from time
    immemorial.
You Yourself are from the everlasting past.
The floods have risen up, O Lord.
The floods have roared like thunder;
the floods have lifted their pounding waves.
But mightier than the violent raging of the seas,
mightier than the breakers on the shore—
the Lord above is mightier than these! (Ps. 93:1–4,
    niv)

To Him be all honor and glory now and forever!

September 7

Increase our faith!

—Luke 17:5, nasb

The apostles said to the Lord, "Increase our faith."

It was a genuine plea. They needed the faith necessary for the radical forgiveness Jesus had just demanded of them. "And if he [your brother] sins against you seven times a day, and returns to you seven times, saying, 'I repent,' forgive him."

I boldly approach You, Lord, and ask that You increase my capacity to forgive.

Increase my faith.

Increase my trust in You.
Increase my hope, my joy, my praise.
Increase my humility, my wisdom.
Increase my courage and integrity.
Increase my knowledge.
Oh, yes, Lord! Increase my love.

> Now to Him who is able to keep you from stumbling, and to make you stand in the presence of His glory blameless with great joy, to the only God our Savior, through Jesus Christ our Lord, be glory, majesty, dominion and authority, before all time and now and forever. Amen.
>
> —Jude 1:24–25, NASB

September 8

> Great is our Lord and mighty in power;
> His understanding has no limit.
>
> —Psalm 147:5, NIV

We can live a triumphant Christian life by plugging into the Power, and that infinite power is ours because it is His. With faith we behold God's wisdom and omnipotence, to whom nothing is impossible or difficult. His power works in us moment by moment by His boundless goodness and His willingness to provide for us every good thing according to His will.

We must stay plugged in. That's our part. And when we do, the current of His almighty power enables us to be victorious in any difficulty.

Where we fail is believing we can overcome challenges by our own power. Independence from God is unplugging the power. It is turned off—a Power-less rather than Power-full Christian life.

> His Spirit made the heavens beautiful, and His
>   power pierced the gliding serpent.
> These are just the beginning of all that He does,
>   merely a whisper of His power.
> Who, then, can comprehend the thunder of His
>   power? (Job 26:13–14, NLT)

September 9

I receive many prayer requests from friends and family. Praying for others has become a priority for me.

However, I don't always know the specific needs of those for whom I have been asked to pray.

The Caim Prayer seeks God's intervention in whatever the circumstances might be—protection, hope, light and peace. I have taken it to memory, which helps me recite it often throughout the day as I remember them to Our Father.

> Circle ____, Lord,
> Keep protection near and danger afar.
> Keep hope within and despair without.
> Keep light near and darkness afar.
> Keep peace within and anxiety without.
> Eternal Father, Son, and Holy Spirit, shield ____
> on every side.

September 10

> Great crowds came to Him, bringing the lame, the
> blind, the crippled, the mute and many others, and
> laid them at His feet; and He healed them.
>
> —Matthew 15:30, NIV

They brought their loved ones to Jesus, laid them at His feet, and He healed them.
  The mute spoke,
  the crippled were restored,
  the blind could see.
  He healed their physical disabilities.

But even greater than this, when the paralytic was brought to Him, He demonstrated the power of forgiveness of sins.

Oh, Lord, what good is a healthy physical body if my soul is sick with sin?

Doctors can treat my physical ailments and disabilities, but only You can
  forgive my sins,
  restore my broken life,
  and make me whole again.
Heal me, Lord!

September 11

> He will deliver the needy who cry out,
>   the afflicted who have no one to help.
>
> —Psalm 72:12, NIV

Child, how needy are you? What burden are you carrying? What grievous sorrow or fear of the future is darkening your path or testing your faith in Me? What do you need this very hour?

I will deliver the needy; I will deliver you. Your human incompleteness meets My divine completeness, and there your deepest yearning is found in Me.

When you have exhausted your earthly options, I will strengthen you with My grace. For when you are weak and weary, I bend down, lifting you above all that troubles you.

As a father cares for his troubled child I care for you.

Come to Me now, give it all to Me, and I will release you from what hinders you from leading a joyful life. I will be your joy.

Don't give *up*; give *in* to Him.

September 12

> Do not be afraid of the nations there,
> for the Lord your God will fight for you.
>
> —Deuteronomy 3:22, NLT

Moses was to encourage and equip Joshua in conquering the remaining forces in the Promised Land. Moses would be denied leading His people to the land "flowing with milk and honey."

Here Moses is recounting the victories won so far and assuring Joshua, "You can do it! You have seen all that the Lord your God has done. Don't be afraid, the Lord is the one fighting for you."

Our battles may not be against evil armies, but don't they seem just as real when faced with fearful circumstances?

I have an urgent need that is impossible to resolve with human effort. There was a time in my walk of faith that I would have fretted and stressed to the point that it consumed me.

But although the problem looms large, I have come to rely on the God of the impossible. Jesus said, "Humanly speaking, it is impossible. But with God everything is possible" (Matt. 19:26, NLT).

He promises that through His mighty power at work within me, He will accomplish infinitely more than I might think or ask.

So why would I not let Him? I know He is fighting for me.

Is there any battle too great for Him? He will equip us, gird us, and lead us. Alone, the magnitude of the battle appears ominous. God has promised to fight with us. But we must let Him.

September 13

> Don't be drunk with wine, because that will ruin
> your life. Instead, be filled with the Holy Spirit.
>
> —Ephesians 5:18, NLT

What did the apostle Paul mean when he commanded believers to be filled with the Spirit? You will note that he contrasts being drunk with wine and being filled with the Spirit. I believe the answer to our question does not lie in the contrast but in the comparison.

A drunken person is controlled by the alcohol within him. The result is that he acts in ways that are normally unnatural to him.

Similarly, the one who is filled with the Holy Spirit acts in ways that are unnatural to the old nature. Instead of impatience, for example, there is self-control. Instead of selfishness, there is consideration of others. Instead of greed, there is generosity.

You understand of course, that the picture Ephesians 5:18 brings to mind is not one of pouring water into a glass until it is full. Rather, since a person full of wine is under its control, so a person filled with the Holy Spirit is controlled by Him. The apostle was therefore telling believers to be controlled by the Holy Spirit.[17]

September 14

> The Lord said, "If you had faith like a mustard
> seed, you would say to this mulberry tree,
> 'Be uprooted and be planted in the sea'; and it
> would obey you."
>
> —Luke 17:6, NASB

Jesus tells His disciples that the least amount of faith can grow. The mustard seed is initially small, but it will take root underground, spread, and then break through the earth.

Like the tiny seed, even a miniscule amount of genuine faith in God will grow. Slowly, almost unnoticeable, this tiny seed becomes a large bush or maybe even a tree.

The seed of faith is planted in our hearts when we accept Christ. It may be so tiny that it is invisible at first, maybe even to ourselves. But it grows as it is watered and cared for. We tend to our faith by staying in God's Word and following His commandments.

Jesus tells of the immeasurable power of faith. He assures us that because of our faith, He enables us to do more than we can imagine. Our faith rests not on our wisdom, but on the power of God.

Plant the seed and watch it grow!

> Fixing our eyes on Jesus, the author and perfecter
> of faith, who for the joy set before Him endured
> the cross, despising the shame, and has sat down at
> the right hand of the throne of God.
>
> —Hebrews 12:2, NASB

September 15

We had counted on the PT scan that would assess the results of the first three chemotherapy treatments that my brother-in-law had completed. Kevin's pain level made it impossible for him to lie flat on his back for the test. It was cancelled and rescheduled when they would first administer drugs to relieve the pain. My sister Judy, Kevin, and I drove home in silence, stunned and disappointed. We had waited weeks for the scan.

When God seems distant and we have more questions than answers, where do we turn?

I come to this quiet place, kneel by my bed, open my Bible and listen to You, O Lord. Your Word revives me.

You tell me You are my comforter in my affliction.

Though my spirit is overwhelmed within me, You know my path.

Give heed to my cry; answer me quickly, O Lord, for my spirit fails. Do not hide Your face from me.

Let me hear Your lovingkindness, for I trust in You. I lift up my soul.

You heal the brokenhearted and bandage our wounds.

While still on my knees, I hear the phone. Judy taps on my door to tell me that the doctor called, and he will be admitting Kevin to the hospital tomorrow where they will administer the drugs and get the scan! We share hugs and praise!

When I am overwhelmed, You alone know the way I should turn, O Lord.

"Now to Him who is able to do far more abundantly beyond all that we ask or think, according to the power that works within us" (Eph. 3:20, NASB).

> Pray for great things, expect great things, work for great things, but above all, pray.
>
> —R. A. Torrey

September 16

> God said to him, 'You fool! You will die this very night. Then who will get everything you worked for?
>
> —Luke 12:20, NIV

Cherry picking time! When growing up, my sisters and I sat around the kitchen table and spent hours pitting cherries. We used bobby pins to dig out the stubborn pits while messy red juice ran down our arms. It was a tiring and seemingly endless job. But it was necessary for us to make provisions for the winter to fill the root cellar that would feed our large family.

It is necessary to make provisions. We are obligated to provide for our families and ourselves. But in this reading Jesus refers to excess as greed. In the parable Jesus tells of a man of wealth who didn't know what to do with all his possessions. He reasoned that he would tear down his barns and build bigger ones. He was proud of all he had achieved and certain that he had many years left to enjoy all he had acquired. He would take it easy—eat, drink, and be merry. Jesus called him a fool, storing up riches for himself but not rich toward God.

There is a big difference between filling a dirt cellar with winter provisions and the barns referred to in today's reading. If the man had too much, why didn't he share a portion with those in need? Greed?

Jesus tells us, "Beware, and be on your guard against every form of greed; for not *even* when one has an abundance does his life consist of his possessions" (Luke 12:15).

Lord, make me a frugal, not possessive, servant.

September 17

I am facing a day that promises to be riddled with challenges that I don't want to tackle. Right now the prospect of it all leaves me weary before I even have my morning coffee.

I sit here with You and open my Bible. You speak to me through Your Word, assuring me that You will be with me through it all. Your power and unfailing love will be my counselor, directing me where I should walk and what words I will say. You are my almighty God, and I greet what is ahead because Your power is behind me!

> But as for me, I will sing about Your power.
> Each morning I will sing with joy about Your unfailing love,
> for You have been my Refuge,
> a place of safety when I am in distress.
> O my Strength, to You I sing praises,
> the God who shows me unfailing love. (Ps. 59:16–17, NLT)

September 18

Ponderings:

- "In three words I can sum up everything I've learned about life: it goes on" (Robert Frost).
- "The problem with a 'living sacrifice' is that it keeps wanting to crawl off the altar" (Jess Phillips).
- "To get the full value of joy, you must have someone to divide it with" (Mark Twain).

- "God cannot give us peace apart from Himself" (C. S. Lewis).
- "If you can solve your problem, then what is the need of worrying. If you cannot solve it, then what is the use of worrying?" (Tulku Thondup)
- "We can see the smoke of a burning home, but who can know of a burning heart?" (Malay saying)
- "What wound did ever heal but by degrees" (William Shakespeare).

September 19

> By His divine power, God has given us everything
> we need for living a godly life. We have received
> all of this by coming to know Him, the One who
> called us to Himself by means of His marvelous
> glory and excellence.
>
> —2 Peter 1:3, NLT

Child, My grace and peace are multiplied as My divine power gives you all things that pertain to life and godliness. Because I love you, I have given you exceedingly great and precious promises. By glory and virtue, you partake in My divine nature, escaping the burdens of self.

Don't waste time dwelling on those faults and failings that can only be overcome by My grace and power. If you set so much importance on your own efforts to conquer them, you are not listening to Me.

Listen to what I have to say. Fling open the window of your mind and let Me speak to you. In time you will find that in quietly listening to Me and not concentrating on yourself, where the fault used to be will be gone. It may happen ever so gradually that it goes unnoticed. But you will see the progress. I will strengthen you in a direction that you weren't aware was the root of the fault.

And when this happens, you will know that I, the almighty God, care for you beyond all that you can know.

> How sweet your words taste to me;
> they are sweeter than honey.
>
> —Psalm 119:103, NLT

September 20

> If you give special attention and a good seat to
> the rich person, but you say to the poor one, "You
> can stand over there, or else sit on the floor"—
> well, doesn't this discrimination show that your
> judgments are guided by evil motives?
>
> —James 2:1–4, NLT

Child, I do not show favoritism, but I accept the one who fears Me and does what is right.

And likewise, believers in Me must not show favoritism. For example, suppose someone comes into your meeting dressed in fancy clothes and expensive jewelry and another comes in who is poor and dressed in dirty clothes.

If you show special attention to the man wearing fine clothes and say, "Here's a good seat for you," but say to the poor man, "You stand there" or "Sit on the floor by my feet," have you not discriminated among yourselves and become judges with evil thoughts?

If you call Me Lord, then you must live as I have commanded; showing no favoritism regardless of appearance. I show no partiality.

Can we honestly say we are not influenced by someone's appearance? Does it affect our reaction toward them? Do we question the attire someone may be wearing when attending church? Do they meet our "criteria" for the proper dress at Sunday service?

"Do not judge or you too will be judged," says the Lord.

Judgment of others leaves no time to judge ourselves. We need to spend our time more wisely.

September 21

> O God, we give glory to You all day long and
> constantly praise Your name!
>
> —Psalm 44:8, NLT

Your love, Lord, reaches to the heavens, Your faithfulness to the skies.

Your righteousness is like the highest mountains,

Your justice like the great deep.

Lord, You preserve both people and animals.

Your unfailing love is priceless!

I take refuge in the shadow of Your wings. I feast on the abundance of Your house.

You give me drink from Your river of delights.

For with You is the fountain of life; in Your light I see light (Ps. 36:5–9, NIV)

Almighty God,

The dawn breaks open with Your glory!

Creation sings of Your Majesty.

Oh Lord, I immerse myself in the wonder of You, the God who made heaven and earth and dwells in me! Alleluia!

September 22

Second nature. According to *Webster*, *second nature* is something that is so familiar that it is done without having to think about it.

I want my relationship with the Lord to be second nature to me, like breathing in and breathing out.

I want it to be second nature for me to live only for Him, counting nothing of this world as more important than Him.

I want it to be second nature that I please Him in all I do, never to commit the smallest act that would offend Him.

I want it be second nature to me that I am always thinking about Him, and my heart continually fixed on Him, and not the things of this world.

To do this, I have to contend with my sinful nature so it will not control me. When I commit to this relationship with Him, the Spirit works in me to control my mind. My sinful nature is always hostile to God and can never please Him. I cannot give it a foothold in my life.

By the power of the Spirit living in us, we can put to death the deeds of our sinful nature.

We can surrender our sinful nature; our second nature nullifies it.

September 23

We are selective about Jesus' teachings. We read through them in the four gospels. Some are good stories, and some we brush over with "That doesn't apply to me."

Jesus sat down near the collection box in the temple and watched as the crowds dropped in their money. Many rich people put in large amounts. Then a poor widow came and dropped in two small coins.

Jesus called His disciples to Him and said, "I tell you the truth, this poor widow has given more than all the others who are making contributions. For they gave a tiny part of their surplus, but she, poor as she is, has given everything she had to live on" (Mark 12:41–44, NLT)

We ask, "How does this apply to me?"

> If you believe what you like in the Gospel, and reject what you do not like, it is not the Gospel you believe, but yourselves.

> —St. Augustine

September 24

> I assure You that I will guide you along the best
> pathway for your life. And I will advise you and
> watch over you.
>
> —Psalm 32:8, NLT

Child, to whom might you turn for counsel and instruction?

You turn to those who are seeking it themselves.

They are troubled and worried about what concerns them.

They may love you and want to help, but they have problems of their own.

Why not ask Me?

I am here for you, loving you more than anyone possibly can.

I will instruct you and teach you in what you should do.

I will show you the way.

My eye is always upon you.

Come to Me, and I will counsel you.

> Commit yourself wholeheartedly
> to these words of Mine.
>
> —Deuteronomy 11:18, NLT

September 25

> Do everything without grumbling or arguing.
>
> —Philippians 2:14, NIV

Child, nothing positive is ever accomplished by complaining or arguing. Has anything you wanted brought positive results by complaining? Whose mind have you changed by arguing? Imitate Me in all that you do.

When throngs eager for My attention left Me tired and weary, I didn't complain.

When challenged by those would have Me killed, I wasn't drawn into arguing. I said what was true and right. It was up to them to reject it or accept it.

I didn't retaliate when I was insulted nor threaten revenge when I suffered. I left this in My Father's hands, who always judges fairly.

I call you to live as a bright light in this world. This light within you produces what is good and right and true.

And those whose intention is to argue and complain will be exposed when the light shines on them, for the light makes everything visible. Live your life following My example. You will reap the benefits of peace and serenity.

September 26

> According to the working of His mighty power
> which He worked in Christ when He raised Him
> from the dead and seated *Him* at His right hand in
> the heavenly *places.*
>
> —Ephesians 1:19–20, NKJV

The power of God surpasses our ability to fathom it. No request is beyond His power to meet. Are we living in the natural or the supernatural?

The story is told of a church that had to begin its Sunday morning service without the music of the organ. As the organist began to play, no music came forth from the instrument. The time necessary for repair was estimated, and a note sent up to the pastor saying, "The power will be on after your morning prayer."

Prayer makes a difference between operating in man's power or God's power.

God's prayer room is always open to those in need. His telephone line is in service twenty-four hours a day. Our line to Him is never busy. No matter how many are praying at the same time, He never misses one prayer.[18]

September 27

> Ah Lord God! Behold, You have made the heavens
> and the earth by Your great power and by Your
> outstretched arm! Nothing is too difficult for You.
>
> —Jeremiah 32:17, NASB

You are faithful to me because I love You. You are loving and care about all that concerns me.

You keep my feet on solid ground when I begin to sink with anxious thoughts.

You lift me above the waves of doubt that grab me, dragging me into the depths of fear.

Troubles surround me, and I cling to You.

You are powerful, and there is nothing You can't do.

I will trust in You.

Right now I surrender to Your strong hand.

Praise You, Lord, God of Heaven's Armies!

> We pray Thee, grant us strength to take
> Our daily cross, whatever it may be,
> And gladly for Thine own dear sake
> In paths of pain to follow Thee. (W. W. How)

September 28

Jesus says the Kingdom of heaven is like a landowner who went out early one morning to hire workers for his vineyard. He agreed to pay the normal daily wage. At 9:00 a.m. and again at 3:00 p.m., as well as at 5:00 p.m., he did the same thing.

In the evening he paid everyone a full day's wage. Those hired first assumed they would receive more. After all, they had worked all day. They protested to the owner. "Hey, those people worked only one hour, and yet you've paid them as much as us; we worked all day in the scorching heat!"

He answered, "Friend, I haven't been unfair! Didn't you agree to work all day for the usual wage? Take your money and go. I wanted to pay this last worker the same as you. Is it against the law for me to do what I want with my money? Should you be jealous because I am kind to others?' So those who are last now will be first then, and those who are first will be last" (Matt. 20:1–16, NLT).

In this parable God is the landowner, and believers are the laborers. It is a powerful teaching about grace; the entrance to the kingdom of heaven is God's grace.

For example, some find Jesus at a young age and commit their life to serving Him. Others come to know Him and follow Him as they age.

Some live a life of self-indulgence, driven by their human nature. They don't acknowledge God or salvation. But when facing death they might call on Him. They may be like the criminal who repented as he was dying on the cross. He turned to Christ for forgiveness, and Christ accepted him.

Our lives will be much more fulfilling and useful if we turn to God early, but even those who repent at the last minute will be saved.

Christ told the dying criminal, "Today you will be with Me in Paradise." We should not begrudge those who turn to God in the last moments of life; none of us deserve eternal life. It is God's gift of grace, unmerited favor, that swings open wide the gates of heaven to all who turn to Him. No one is too late!

September 29

> Do not fear, for I am with you; do not
> anxiously look about you, for I am your God.
> I will strengthen you, surely I will help you; surely
> I will uphold you with My righteous right hand.
>
> —Isaiah 41:10, NASB

I experience Your victory at times when I least expect it. It is like discovering a valuable gem in a messy drawer.

I recognize victory when I hold my tongue rather than say what I think. Victory is mine when I withhold judgment rather than criticize. I know victory when I look beyond disturbances that irritate me.

Those times aren't always easy for me. But victory comes with discipline. And with the practice of discipline I am able to move past so much that would normally aggravate me.

With each small victory I become more aware of Your power in me. I certainly can't do this on my own. My humanness demands that I respond negatively.

We must discipline ourselves to overcome the enemy, Satan. He never lets up, always drawing us into conflict. Because God provides us the power and grace, we can claim victory in His name when we conquer nagging temptations. We can rejoice in each victory because we know it comes ultimately from Him who upholds us with His righteous right hand. He delights in our victories!

September 30

> The Word became flesh and made His dwelling among us. We have seen His glory, the glory of the one and only Son, who came from the Father, full of grace and truth.
>
> —John 1:14, NIV

As God's grace changes our heart and cleanses and sanctifies us, we can see the evidence of the change.

We begin to grow in love, to forget self, and live for others. It's gradual; we may not see it at first. But subtly our thoughts drift more toward heaven, and we are content to spend time just thinking of Him. We linger longer in His Word. It alters our perception of what's important.

Such change brings peace to the hardest days.

And all of this, as blessed as it is, is just the beginning. We continue to grow and change as God's grace supplies what is required to die to self and live only for Him. He will supply all our needs according to His riches. We will be changed!

> Out of His fullness we have all received
> grace in place of grace already given.
>
> —John 1:16, NIV

October 1

Jesus entered Jericho and made His way through the town. There was a man there named Zacchaeus. He was the chief tax collector in the region, and he had become very rich. He tried to get a look at Jesus but was too short to see over the crowd. So he ran ahead and climbed a sycamore fig tree beside the road knowing Jesus was going to pass that way.

When Jesus came by, He looked up and saw Zacchaeus. He called him by name. "Zacchaeus! Quick, come down! I must be a guest in your home today."

Jubilant, Zacchaeus scrambled down the tree and took Jesus to his house. But the people were displeased. "He has gone to be the guest of a notorious sinner," they grumbled,

Meanwhile, Zacchaeus stood before the Lord and said, "I will give half my wealth to the poor, Lord, and if I have cheated people on their taxes, I will give them back four times as much!"

Jesus responded, "Salvation has come to this home today, for this man has shown himself to be a true son of Abraham. For the Son of Man came to seek and save those who are lost" (Luke 19:1—10, NLT).

When Jesus calls you, respond!

October 2

> You have granted him unending blessings, and
> made him glad with the joy of Your presence.
>
> —Psalm 21:6, NIV

The fullness of joy is to behold God in all things. He gives us everything, which we enjoy now and eternally. We reap the joys of life when we partake in His majesty. We sing songs of praise when we open ourselves to all He has given and all He will give. We come before Him with:

> LORD, You alone are my inheritance, my cup of blessing.
> You guard all that is mine.
> The land You have given me is a pleasant land.
> What a wonderful inheritance!
> I will bless the LORD who guides me;
> even at night my heart instructs me.
> I know the LORD is always with me.
> I will not be shaken, for He is right beside me.
> No wonder my heart is glad, and I rejoice.
> My body rests in safety.
> For You will not leave my soul among the dead
> or allow Your holy one to rot in the grave.
> You will show me the way of life,
> granting me the joy of Your presence
> and the pleasures of living with You forever. (Ps. 16:5–11, NIV)

October 3

> Do you not know? Have you not heard? The Everlasting God, the Lord, the Creator of the ends

> of the earth does not become weary or tired. His
> understanding is inscrutable. He gives strength
> to the weary, and to him who lacks might He
> increases power. Though youths grow weary and
> tired, and vigorous young men stumble badly,
> yet those who wait for the Lord will gain new
> strength; they will mount up with wings like
> eagles, they will run and not get tired, they will
> walk and not become weary.
>
> —Isaiah 40:28–31, NASB

One chore I particularly disliked while growing up on the farm was pulling milkweeds. My sisters and I would spread out and head down the couple acres of alfalfa, pulling the pesky weed. After going a short distance and looking behind me, they seemed to be growing as fast as I could pull them! It was discouraging.

Problems are like that. They keep cropping up. When one is resolved, we know there will be more. We will never be free of problems.

Must we plod wearily along believing there is no escape from the burdens? No! We can mount up with wings like eagles if we wait on the Lord instead of trying to solve the problem by ourselves.

The eagle represents freedom. He lives on lofty mountaintops and in the solitary grandeur of nature. He sweeps into valleys below and upward into boundless spaces. He uses thermals, rising currents of warm air, to help him soar. So he needs very little wing flapping, enabling him to conserve energy. Oh, that we would soar like the eagle and allow God to take care of the wearisome problems that disturb us. Test your wings.

Help me to rise above the problems, Lord. I want to soar!

October 4

I watch the protestors lining each side of the roped-off area. "For" on one side. "Against" on the other. Shouts of anger clash in the middle of the street. Each group is passionate, knowing they are right! There seems to be no neutral ground.

I've not participated in a protest, but I admit that while watching some of them on TV, I take sides. I think, *Good for you! That's right!* Sometimes I think, *You have got to be kidding! Do you really believe that?*

I think there's some of a protestor in all of us. We latch on to what we think is right, and there is no neutral ground. It leaves relationships broken and crumbling around us. Sides are drawn, leading to anger and finger-pointing. Even if we love the other side, we refuse to admit that we could be wrong.

Here are some quotes from the *Building Solid Relationships* book.

- Be patient with each other, making allowance for each other's faults because of your love (Eph. 4:2, NLT).
- Get rid of all bitterness, rage, anger, harsh words, and slander. Instead, be kind to each other, tenderhearted, forgiving one another, just as God through Christ has forgiven you (Eph. 4:31–32, NLT).
- Above all, clothe yourselves with love, which binds us all together in perfect harmony (Col. 3:14, NLT).

Harmony results when we blend patience, love, kindness, tenderheartedness, forgiveness, encouragement, admitting our failings to each other, and praying for each other.

No longer protest but protect! Your relationships are worth it.

October 5

> But as many as received Him, to them He gave
> the right to become children of God, to those who
> believe in His name: who were born, not of blood,
> nor of the will of the flesh, nor of the will of man,
> but of God.
>
> —John 1:13, NKJV

Father, I know how much You love me; You call me Your child. The child of the almighty God! You have adopted me, and I call you Abba, Father. I am reborn into Your family, not with a physical birth from human passion or planning, but with a birth that comes from You.

I have not yet seen You physically, but I wait with eager expectation for Your return when I will see You face-to-face. You promise me that I will be like You.

Because You have begun to work in me from the time of my adoption, my life is a process of becoming more and more like You.

I am a sinner, but as a child wants to please her parent, so I want to please You in what I do or say, what I watch on TV, what movies I see, what I read. I strive to be pure as You are pure.

One day I will be at home with You, Abba, Father!

October 6

> Therefore there is now no condemnation for those
> who are in Christ Jesus. For the law of the Spirit of
> life in Christ Jesus has set you free from the law of
> sin and of death.
>
> —Romans 8:1, NASB

Father, because I belong to You, the power of the life giving Spirit has freed me from sin that leads to death. There is no condemnation for me because I belong to You!

You sent Your Son in a body like the body I have. You declared an end to sin's control over me by giving Jesus as a sacrifice for my sins. You did this for me! You find me blameless because He took the blame! How can I begin to comprehend such love?

I sin, Lord, but I am not controlled by sin, for I listen to the Spirit who enables me to resist my sinful nature. I know this to be so because when I give in to the weakness of my flesh, the Spirit penetrates my conscience, and I know that I have sinned against You.

Knowing this, I come immediately to You, telling You that I am truly sorry for what I have done.

The power of Your Spirit working in me brings me to You to confess my sin and ask forgiveness. I am a sinner beyond any human remedy, but I am free from the power and guilt of sin in my life only through the power of the Holy Spirit.

October 7

> So the creation of the heavens and the earth and
> everything in them was completed. On the seventh
> day God had finished His work of creation,
> so He rested from all His work.
>
> —Genesis 2:1–2, NASB

When I was young, every Monday was laundry day. Before the sun came up, the washing machine was rolled off the screened-in back porch onto the blue flowered linoleum kitchen floor. The four-legged machine worked compatibly with two metal washtubs; one filled with rinse water, the other with bluing. The clothes were hung on the five long lines that stretched across the grassy area just outside the back door. When they were dry, we used a Coke bottle with a sprinkler on the end to dampen those that needed to be ironed, rolled them up, and put them in a pillowcase. Tuesday was ironing day.

I learned at a young age if there is an order of things, the work can be accomplished. God is a God of order. He created the heavens and the earth in an orderly fashion. From the first day that He separated the light from the darkness to the seventh day when He rested, there was order. Order brings harmony and tranquility. Chaos brings confusion. God is not a God of confusion but of peace.

Check the order of things in your life. Do you find chaos or tranquility?

Lord, help me to live my life with order.

October 8

Pride rears its ugly head when I least expect it. I hate pride! *Webster's Dictionary* defines it as "inordinate self-esteem; conceit."

The Bible tells us that man's pride will bring him low, but a humble spirit will obtain honor (Prov. 29:23, NASB).

It warns us that pride goes before destruction and haughtiness before a fall (Prov. 16:18, NASB).

As I read God's Word, this sin is ever more glaring. I recognize it in myself all the time. I believe my pride is anything for which I take credit. Pride in my heart separates me from God.

There is nothing I can do to escape the snare of pride. For even thinking that I can do something about it *is* pride. This brings me to the end of myself, and I know I am totally dependent on the Holy Spirit, who alone sees my needs and will reveal and convict me with tender love.

It is only when I am stirred to an understanding of my need for Him that I can seek His help. When I come face-to-face with reality, my reliance on myself is worth nothing.

Pride is sin. How foolish it is to be proud, to exalt myself! I have been created to need God.

Nothing in all creation is hidden from Him. Everything is naked and exposed before His eyes, and He is the one to whom we are accountable (Heb. 4:13, NLT).

October 9

> Trust in the Lord always, for the
> Lord God is the eternal Rock.
>
> —Isaiah 26:4, NLT

We are living out these lives of ours too much apart from God.

We toil on dismally, as if the making or the marring of our destinies rested wholly with ourselves. It is not so.

We are not the lonely, orphaned creatures we let ourselves suppose ourselves to be.

The earth, rolling on its way through space, does not go unattended. The maker and controller of it is with it, and around it, and upon it.

He is with us here and now. He knows us infinitely more thoroughly than we know ourselves. He loves us better than we have ever dared to believe could be possible.[19]

> Heaven consists in nothing else than walking, abiding and resting in the Divine Presence.
>
> —John Pulsford

October 10

The Lord is my shepherd, my best friend.

With Him, I am complete, and there is nothing that I want.

When I am weary or discouraged, He makes me lie down in green pastures.

And when I need to be refreshed and nourished, He leads me beside the quiet, still waters.

He restores my soul.

When I listen to Him and follow Him, He guides me in the paths of righteousness for His name's sake.

When I walk through the troubled valleys in this life, I am not afraid, and when I face the valley of the shadow of death, I will not fear because His rod and His staff will comfort me.

He prepares a feast table for me and protects me from the enemy.

He anoints my head with soothing oil.

My cup is so full it overflows!

I know that goodness and mercy will follow me all the days of my life, and I will live with Him in His house forever (Ps. 23).

October 11

> When they began singing and praising, the Lord
> set ambushes against the sons of Ammon, Moab
> and Mount Seir, who had come against Judah; so
> they were routed.
>
> —2 Chronicles 20:22, NASB

The enemy was fast approaching. King Jehoshaphat was afraid and turned his attention to seek the LORD, and proclaimed a fast throughout all Judah (2 Chron. 20:3, NASB).

God spoke through the prophet Zahaziel, and he said, "Listen, all Judah and the inhabitants of Jerusalem and King Jehoshaphat: thus says the LORD to you, 'Do not fear or be dismayed because of this great multitude, for the battle is not yours but God's'" (2 Chron. 20:15, NASB).

Jehoshaphat bowed his head with his face to the ground, and all Judah and the inhabitants of Jerusalem fell down before the LORD, worshiping the LORD (2 Chron. 20:18, NASB).

He appointed those who sang to the LORD and those who praised Him in holy attire, as they went out before the army and said, "Give thanks to the LORD, for His lovingkindness is everlasting" (2 Chron. 20:21, NASB).

We may not be faced with a mighty army as was the king, but we can be overcome by the enemy, Satan. He is a powerful force of the darkness and wickedness. Alone, we are no match for Him. We need the power of God and the heavenly forces to ward off such an enemy.

When the battle ahead looms ominous, we can fall in line behind the Lord. Do what we are able to: worshiping and singing to the Lord. He can win!

October 12

Child, don't turn your back on wisdom, for she will protect you. Love her, and she will guard you.

And whatever else you do, develop good judgment. If you prize wisdom, she will make you great. Embrace her, and she will honor you. She will place a lovely wreath on your head; she will present you with a beautiful crown (Prov. 4:6–9, NLT).

If you need wisdom, ask Me and I will give it to you. I will not rebuke you for asking. But when you ask Me, be sure that your faith is in Me alone. Do not waver, for a person with divided loyalty is as unsettled as a wave of the sea that is blown and tossed by the wind. Such people should not expect to receive anything from Me (James 1:5–7, NLT).

If you are wise and understand My ways, prove it by living an honorable life, doing good works with the humility that comes from wisdom. But if you are bitterly jealous and there is selfish ambition in your heart, don't cover up the truth with boasting and lying. For jealousy and selfishness are not My kind of wisdom.

But the wisdom from above is first of all pure. It is also peace-loving, gentle at all times, and willing to yield to others. It is full of mercy and the fruit of good deeds. It shows no favoritism and is always sincere (James 3:13–17, NLT).

> Commit yourself wholeheartedly
> to these words of Mine.
>
> —Deuteronomy 11:18, NLT

October 13

> Our purpose is to please God, not people.
> He alone examines the motives of our hearts.
>
> —1 Thessalonians 2:4, NLT

If God has appointed us to a task, He expects us to see it through.

He told His disciples:

> When a servant comes in from plowing or taking care of sheep, does his master say, "Come in and eat with me"? "No," he says, "Prepare my meal, put on

your apron, and serve me while I eat. Then you can
eat later."

And does the master thank the servant for doing
what he was told to do? Of course not. In the same
way, when you obey me you should say, "We are
unworthy servants who have simply done our duty."
(Luke 17:7–10, NLT)

Do we sometimes feel we deserve credit for serving
God? Do we hold positions in the church to bring attention
to ourselves? Do we boast about our community service?

Jesus isn't calling our service meaningless, no more than
He calls the work of the slaves in the field meaningless. He
is calling us to obey without our self-esteem and spiritual
pride on display.

When He has commissioned us for the task, it is our
duty.

And we have abundant assurance that He will supply all
the strength we need to perform any duty God allots to us.

It is a great deal easier to do that which God gives
us to do, no matter how hard it is, than to face the
responsibility of not doing it.

—J. H. Newman

October 14

Child, this morning I desire a few minutes alone with you. In the quiet communion we share, you will know of My constant love for you. It is a love that even your dearest earthly companion can't supply.

I created the universe, and I created you. You are Mine, I am yours. Such love cannot be matched.

Won't you come and sit with Me for awhile? Here you can pour out all that disturbs you, and I will listen.

I will strengthen you and encourage you in any challenge that you will meet today. You will feel the warmth of My love and the power of My grace.

Ask Me, and I will tell you remarkable secrets you do not know about things to come (Jer. 33:3, NLT).

October 15

Jesus went through the towns and villages, teaching as He went, always pressing on toward Jerusalem.

Someone asked Him, "Lord, will only a few be saved?"

He replied, "Work hard to enter the narrow door to God's Kingdom, for many will try to enter but will fail. When the Master of the house has locked the door, it will be too late. You will stand outside knocking and pleading,

'Lord, open the door for us!' But He will reply, 'I don't know you or where you come from.'

Then you will say, 'But we ate and drank with You, and You taught in our streets.' And He will reply, 'I tell you, I don't know you or where you come from. Get away from Me, all you who do evil.

There will be weeping and gnashing of teeth, for you will see Abraham, Isaac, Jacob, and all the prophets in the Kingdom of God, but you will be thrown out.

And people will come from all over the world—from east and west, north and south—to take their places in the Kingdom of God. Some who seem least important now will be the greatest then, and some who are the greatest now will be least important then" (Luke 13:22–30, NLT).

> Does not My Word burn like fire…. is it not like a mighty hammer that smashes a rock to pieces?
>
> —Jeremiah 23:29, NLT

October 16

Father, You have charged me to keep Your commandments carefully. Oh, that my actions would consistently reflect those commands. Then I will not be ashamed to compare my life to what You want me to do.

As I learn Your righteous regulations, I will thank You by living as I should. I will obey Your decrees. Please don't give up on me.

Turn my eyes from worthless things and give me life through Your Word.

Help me to abandon any shameful ways.

Renew my life with Your goodness.

You are close to all who call on You in truth.

You grant the desires of those who fear You.

You hear my cry for help and rescue me.

> It is decreed in the providence of God that, although the opportunities for doing good, which are in the power of every man, are beyond count or knowledge; yet the opportunity once neglected, no man by any self-sacrifice can atone for those who have fallen or suffered by his negligence.
>
> —Juliana H. Ewing

October 17

Sin. We don't like to use that word much. Hearing a sermon on the subject can make us nervous; we look at our watch.

How do we define sin? Is it sin if nobody gets hurt? The Bible's definition is that all sin is contrary to God's law, and if we know what to do and don't do it, we sin.

Paul lays it out with words that are mingled with choices of slavery or freedom. Do not let sin control the way you live; do not give in to sinful desires. Do not let any part of your body become an instrument of evil to serve sin. Instead, give yourselves completely to God, for you were dead, but now you have new life. So use your whole body as an instrument to do what is right for the glory of God.

Sin is no longer your master, for you no longer live under the requirements of the law. Instead, you live under the freedom of God's grace. You can be a slave to sin, which leads to death, or you can choose to obey God, which leads to righteous living (Rom. 6:12–14, 16, NLT).

Sin:

1) Always brings unpleasant consequences.
2) Lest we think the joy of cleansing makes sin worthwhile, think again.
3) The pain of harvest will always exceed the pleasure of sowing. (Charles Swindol)

October 18

> Sing praises to God and to His name! Sing loud
> praises to Him who rides the clouds.
> His name is the Lord—Rejoice in his presence!
> His name is the Lord—rejoice in His presence!
>
> —Psalm 68:4, NLT

Our hearts rejoice and shout the praises of our God. He is ever present in our lives. Moments throughout our day, we can turn our thoughts and hearts toward Him and feel His pleasure. As we discipline ourselves in thinking about Him, the more we think of His Majesty, the Creator of heaven and earth, our hearts leap for joy to know that He is our God! We are His children and He delights in us.

> Praise the Lord; praise God our savior!
> For each day He carries us in his arms.
> Sing to God, you kingdoms of the earth.
> Sing praises to the Lord.
> Sing to the one who rides across the ancient heavens,
> His mighty voice thundering from the sky.
> Tell everyone about God's power. (Ps. 68:32–34, NLT)

> How joyful are those who fear the Lord—
> all who follow His ways!
> You will enjoy the fruit of your labor.
> How joyful and prosperous you will be!
>
> —Psalm 128:1–2, NLT

The all-important thing is not to live apart from God, but as far as possible to be consciously with Him. It must need be that those who look much into His face will become like Him.

—Charles H. Brent

October 19

I've never been a big fan of Proverbs, but as I delve deeper into the book, it does have some sound advice for living, along with consequences of our actions.

- A hard worker has plenty of food, but a person who chases fantasies has no sense (Prov. 12:11, NLT).
- Lazy people want much but get little, but those who work hard will prosper (Prov. 13:4, NLT).
- Wealth from get-rich-quick schemes quickly disappears; wealth from hard work grows over time (Prov. 13:11, NLT).

- Work brings profit, but mere talk leads to poverty! (Prov. 14:23, NLT)
- It is good for workers to have an appetite; an empty stomach drives them on (Prov. 16:26, NLT).
- Good planning and hard work lead to prosperity, but hasty shortcuts lead to poverty (Prov. 21:5, NLT).

God has given us two ends,
One to think with,
One to sit with.
All the success and failure in life depends on which
    end you use.
Heads you win,
Tails you lose! (John Cassis)

October 20

I am the true Grapevine, and my
Father is the Gardener.

—John 15:1, NLT

Child, I am the true Grapevine, and you are the branches. My Father is the gardener, and He cares for you that you might be fruitful.

If you become unproductive, He must cut you off. You are a dead branch and may infect the rest of the branches.

If you are bearing fruit, He will need to occasionally prune you. For as with any tree, fruitful branches are pruned to promote growth.

You have already been pruned and purified by the message I have given you. Remain in Me, and I will remain in you. For a branch cannot produce fruit if it is severed from the vine, and you cannot be fruitful unless you remain in Me. For apart from Me you can do nothing.

Anyone who does not remain in Me is thrown away like a useless branch and withers. Such branches are gathered into a pile to be burned. But if you remain in Me and My words remain in you, you may ask for anything you want, and it will be granted! When you produce much fruit, you are My true disciples. This brings great glory to My Father, the gardener.

You must remember You didn't choose Me. I chose you. I appointed you to go and produce lasting fruit so that the Father will give you whatever you ask for, using My name. This is My command: love each other (John 15:2–17, NLT).

October 21

> Remember Your promise to me; it is my only hope. Your promise revives me; it comforts me in all my troubles.
>
> —Psalm 119:49–50, NLT

I believe that tucked away in our hearts we bear sorrows that no one can see. Hopefully we have that best friend in whom we can confide.

But for the occasional visit with a casual acquaintance, those sorrows are not visible.

We go about our daily routine with our best face on, all the while our heart may be sad; there may be circumstances that trouble us, we may be dealing with health issues for ourselves or loved ones.

Someone asks "How are you?" and our first inclination might be to say, "How much time do you have?" But instead we usually say, "I'm fine, how are you?"

But also I think we have sorrows that can never be told to anyone; we can't even put them into words because sometimes we have emotions that are too deep for expression in articulate language. I experience those times. When I do, I must go to Jesus and lay them wordlessly before Him. He knows my brokenness, and I don't have to speak.

My heart seeks Him, and I find an unexplainable deep peace that settles in—peace not because of understanding, but beyond understanding.

Lord, this *mourning* so deep in my soul is not visible to even those who know me most intimately. It can be heard only by You. I don't seek answers but the will to endure and the determination to trust and know that You, O God, control the universe and will control my helplessness. Thank you, Jesus.

> Walking with a friend in the dark is better than walking alone in the light.

> —Helen Keller

October 22

> I entrust my spirit into Your hand…
> for You are a faithful God.
>
> —Psalm 31:5, NLT

Lord, I come to You for protection.

Turn Your ear to listen to me.

Be my Rock of Protection, a fortress where I will be safe.

I entrust my spirit into Your hand.

My future is in Your hands.

Let Your favor shine on me, and Your unfailing love rescue me.

How great is the goodness You have stored up for those who fear You.

You lavish it on those who come to You for protection, blessing us before the watching world (Ps. 31:19, NLT).

You hide me in the shelter of Your presence.

Praise You Lord, for You have shown me the wonders of Your unfailing love.

I will be strong and courageous, putting all my hope in You.

> To Thee I bring my care,
> The care I cannot flee,
> Thou wilt not only share,
> But bear it all for me.
> O loving Saviour, now to Thee
> I bring the load that wearies me. (Frances R. Havergal)

October 23

Father, You created me, and I want to please You. I have my hope in You, whose unfailing love comforts me.

Each day brings new challenges. I can feel strong when I meet them, but then I falter and fail. Waves of doubt and fear wash over me. You know that about me. But You also know how much I love You and need to depend on You and not on myself. Give me a discerning mind. Sustain me.

Today will bring the unexpected. So I prepare myself, beginning it with gratitude for Your abundant blessings, allowing my heart to overflow with my love for You.

I bask in the radiance of Your glory. I experience the joy of Your presence. I am confident that nothing that happens will shake me. As You surround me with Your tender mercies, I will rise above whatever tries to bring me down.

Doubt will be replaced with certainty, and fear with trust. I am prepared to meet the day!

> I have set the Lord always before me. Because He
> is at my right hand, I will not be shaken.
>
> —Psalm 16:8, NLT

October 24

Child, by My divine power I have given you everything you need to live a godly life. All that you have received is yours because I have called you to Myself.

Through My marvelous glory and excellence you have come to know Me. I have given you great and precious promises. My power flows through you so that you are able to escape the worldly corruption caused by human desires (2 Pet. 1:3–4, NLT).

You will grow and be productive and useful in living a godly life, fulfilling the plans I have for You.

Do you not know? Have you not heard? I am the everlasting God, the Lord, the creator of the ends of the earth. I never grow weary or tired. No one can measure the depth of My understanding.

I will give you strength for everything that comes your way, and if you feel powerless, I will increase your power.

You are My child; what is Mine is yours (Isa. 40:28–29, NLT).

October 25

We think Jonah's story of being swallowed by a great fish is pretty far-fetched. God told him to go to Nineveh and Jonah said, "No!" He went in the opposite direction to get away from the Lord and boarded a ship heading for Tarshish.

I believe Jonah's story is lodged in scripture to show us that we can't get away from the Lord. And when we try, we suffer consequences that take us to a deep and dark place. Escape is impossible until we cry to the Lord to save us. Jonah did.

Here's Jonah's prayer:

> I cried out to the Lord in my great trouble, and He answered me. I called to You from the land of the dead, and Lord, You heard me!
>
> You threw me into the ocean depths, and I sank down to the heart of the sea. The mighty waters engulfed me; I was buried beneath Your wild and stormy waves…

I sank beneath the waves, and the waters closed over me. Seaweed wrapped itself around my head. I sank down to the very roots of the mountains. I was imprisoned in the earth, whose gates lock shut forever.

But You, O Lord my God, snatched me from the jaws of death!

As my life was slipping away, I remembered the Lord.

Those who worship false gods turn their backs on all God's mercies. But I will offer sacrifices to You with songs of praise, and I will fulfill all my vows. (Jon. 2:1–9, NLT)

October 26

"I had a biopsy and am waiting for the results. Please pray it's not cancer!"

I could see her doubt and worry as she asked for prayer from those she knew would respond.

So how do we pray for her while waiting for the results?

I pray that God's will be done in her life.

If it is benign, I praise Him for His answer, just as the leper returned thanking Jesus, who cherishes a grateful heart.

If malignant, I pray for discernment by capable and caring physicians.

I pray for her protection, hope, light, and peace. Abide in her, Lord!

And I pray that God's Word is embedded in her heart.

> Quality prayer is prayer that seeks God first and answers second.
>
> —Dick Eastman

> One of the greatest trials and miseries of this life seems to me to be the absence of a grand spirit to keep the body under control. Illness and grievous afflictions, though they are a trial, I think nothing of, if the soul is strong, for it praises God, and sees that everything comes from His hand.
>
> —St. Teresa

October 27

> Worship the Lord.
>
> —Psalm 29:2, NLT

The earth and all that is in it belongs to You, O Lord. You laid the foundation of the sea, and built it on the ocean depths.

As I walk along the shores of the blue Pacific, there mingles such depth of feelings in me that I cannot begin to sort through them.

Wordless Worship!

Awesome Adoration!

Peaceful Praise!

Your majesty speaks to me through the wonder of the powerful motion that brings sweeping waves to meet me. Whatever burdens I have brought here with me are swept away!

> Honor the Lord for the glory of His name.
> Worship the Lord in the splendor of His holiness.
> The voice of the Lord echoes above the sea.
> The God of glory thunders. (Ps. 29:2–3, NLT)

October 28

> So be strong and courageous, all you
> who put your hope in the Lord!
>
> —Psalm 31:24, NLT

Ernest Hemingway wrote, "Courage is fear that has prayed." Yet Hemingway took his own life in despair.

Our troubles may not be our biggest difficulty but, instead, our reaction to them. If we believe that the only means we have for a resolution is within ourselves, we probably will despair.

When we come to the end of all our own resources, in our brokenness we can find the power of God who will sustain us and do what we cannot do. An anonymous quote says, "It takes more courage to be faithful in routine things than to risk one's life in a moment of spectacular danger."

Do we agree with that? It is a single physical act of courage to jump into a raging river to rescue a drowning man. It is moral courage—fortitude—to be a 24/7 caregiver for an elderly parent or to be a single parent.

Courage is rooted in the conviction that God is enough. When we know that, we face the future not with despair, but knowing we are in His loving care.

> Courage is resistance to fear, mastery of fear—not absence of fear.
>
> —Mark Twain

October 29

Ticktock! Ticktock! Ticktock!

The new wall clock in my prayer corner fills the silent room with its rhythmic sound of passing time. It's loud. I ordered it online for its outdoors look: the décor of the sunroom. It was a good find, and I don't want to return it. I've decided I can live with its noisy company.

Sitting here listening to the clock that shares my space, I am reminded how precious each minute of my life can be. I want to maximize my time, use it wisely, and make a difference.

> I have only just a minute,
> Only sixty seconds in it.
> Forced upon me, can't refuse it,
> Didn't seek it,
> Didn't choose it,
> But it's up to me to use it.
> I must suffer if I lose it,
> Give account if I abuse it.
> Just a tiny little minute
> But an eternity is in it! (Dr. Benjamin Mays)

October 30

> You shall love the Lord your God with all your
> heart, with all your soul, and with all your mind.
> This is the first and great commandment.
>
> —Matthew 22:37, NKJV

I've read that during their time in the womb, babies hear, feel, and even smell their mothers. They are bonded with the mother before birth.

But adoptive parents will tell you that biology is only part of the love story. Young babies bond emotionally with people who give them regular care and affection. In fact, the first step in ensuring that your baby will bond with others is to attend to her needs in a timely fashion and let her know that she's loved.

Emotions of love come naturally to the newborn and parent. But loving God is a commandment.

To me, it is simple. I am the third child born to my parents, and we bonded right from birth. I love my earthly parents, and they love me.

But biology is only part of this love story.

I am a child of God, adopted when I accepted Jesus as my Savior. And so I received God's Spirit when He adopted me as His own child. He is Abba, Father.

Since I was adopted by Him, I have bonded with Him emotionally. He has given me constant care and affection. He has attended to all my needs in a timely fashion.

I came to know my adopted Father later in my life. But how the love has grown! It started with an acknowledgement of His love and the awareness of His tender love for me.

I look forward to the day when I will be with my earthly parents and my Heavenly Father in His heavenly kingdom.

"For we know that when this earthly tent we live in is taken down (that is, when we die and leave this earthly body), we will have a house in heaven, an eternal body made for us by God Himself and not by human hands" (2 Cor. 5:1, NLT).

October 31

I first read this when I was a young mother. I believe I am better now about leaving my cares to Him, but I still have a tendency to snatch them back. God seems slow when I just want Him to fix it now!

> As children bring their broken toys
> with tears for us to mend,
> I brought my broken dreams to God,
> because He was my friend.
> But, then, instead of leaving Him

in peace to work alone,
I hung around and tried to help,
with ways that were my own.
At last I snatched them back and cried,
"How can you be so slow?"
"My child," He said,
"What could I do? You never did let go." (Author
unknown)

> Wait patiently for the Lord. Be brave and
> courageous. Yes, wait patiently for the Lord.
>
> —Psalm 27:14

November 1

> I find My heart is confident in You O God; no
> wonder I can sing Your praises with all my heart!
>
> —Psalm 108:1, NLT

I have just learned some disturbing news. I am shaken; I
need to talk to someone. I open my Bible to psalms of praise.

You ask, who can list the glorious miracles of the Lord?
Who can ever praise Him enough?" (Ps. 106:2, NLT)

In Psalm 103:1–2 (NLT) You instruct me to praise You
with all that I am, to praise You with all my heart, and

praise Your Holy Name. I am to never forget the good things You do for me.

"Come let us sing to the Lord! Let us shout joyfully to the Rock of our Salvation. Let us come to Him with thanksgiving and sing psalms of praise to Him" (Ps. 95:1–3, NLT).

You, O Lord, are a great God, a great King above all gods. Praise lifts us above the circumstances. It brings us into God's presence, lifting us to a place of repose and rest. It is an amazing remedy for an anxious heart.

Try praise!

November 2

Ponderings on Prayer:

- "Prayer does not just fit us for the greater work. Prayer is the greater work" (Oswald Chambers).
- "What wings are to a bird, and sails to a ship, is prayer to the soul" (Corrie Ten Boom).
- "If I feel myself disinclined to pray, then is the time when I need to pray more than ever. Possibly when the soul leaps and exults in communion with God, it might more safely refrain from prayer than at those seasons when it drags heavily in devotion" (Charles H. Spurgeon).

- "It is better to pray from the heart without words than to pray words without heart" (John Bunyan).
- "When in prayer you clasp your hands, God opens His" (German proverb).
- "Prayer is the power that wields the weapon of the Word" (John Piper).
- "A day hemmed in prayer seldom unravels" (Anonymous).

November 3

Child, I oppose the proud and favor the humble. Humble yourself under My mighty power, and when it is the right time, I will lift you up in honor. This is My promise to you; I always take care of you.

Give all your worries and cares to Me. Why would you carry such a load when I will do it for You?

Stay alert! Watch out for the great enemy, the devil. He prowls around like a roaring lion looking for someone to devour. Stand firm against him and be strong in your faith.

Remember, My loved one, that your Christian brothers and sisters all over the world are going through the same kind of suffering that you are.

In My kindness, I have called you to share in My eternal glory by means of My Son, Jesus. So after you have suffered a little while, I will restore, support, and strengthen you, and I will place you on a firm foundation (1 Pet. 5:5–11, NLT).

In perplexities—when we cannot tell what to do, when we cannot understand what is going on around us, let us be calmed and steadied and made patient by the thought that what is hidden from us is not hidden from Him.

—Frances Ridley Havergal

November 4

If a man will not work, he shall not eat.

—2 Thessalonians 3:10, NASB

One of my favorite early-morning farm chores while growing up was gathering eggs. Pushing open the creaky wooden door always sent the hens into a cackling uproar.

But I ignored their protest. Moving down the row of straw-filled wooden cubbyholes, I wrestled my hand under the warm breast of the chicken to gather her eggs.

I was raised in a family with nine siblings. My sisters and I shared everything, from beds to clothes. And we shared the work. We were expected from an early age to participate in daily chores. We learned a good work ethic that has contributed to a productive life for all of us.

Thomas Edison said, "Opportunity is missed by most people because it's dressed in overalls and looks like work."

Paul's letter is clear. If you don't work, you don't eat. He addresses those who are lazy and undisciplined. Instead of working, they spend time being busybodies. Idle time can lead to unhealthy habits.

Even if we are no longer in the workforce, there are countless opportunities to spend time helping others. Engage in productive activity.

Thank you for the ability to work and contribute, Lord.

November 5

> I came that they may have life,
> and have it abundantly.
>
> —John 10:10, NASB

Webster's defines abundant as "more than adequate, plentiful."

Hetty Green lived in the early 1900s and is described as a wealthy woman who lived like a pauper. She was an American businesswoman, a savvy financier, and one of the first women to turn a fortune on Wall Street.

She was often seen plodding alone up and down Wall Street in her faded black dress, dirty and ragged at the seams. She carried a case with her: a pitiful lunch tossed inside, usually graham crackers or dry oatmeal. She frequently traveled a considerable distance to a grocery store that sold broken cookies that were cheaper.

When she died in 1916 she was considered the wealthiest woman in America. She had the resources to live well, but she didn't use them.

We have all the resources readily available to live an abundant life when we know God. It's not necessarily a life of wealth or what the world has to offer. It is access to extravagant resources God can provide. But some Christians don't access all that God has supplied in Christ. Like Hetty and her money, we are spiritually wealthy but live like spiritual paupers.

The secret to this abundant life is a close relationship with God when we follow the truths in His Word. Without that, we can end up like Hetty, dressed in dirty and ragged clothes, eating a meager diet. How foolish we can be! Spiritually starving and letting this go to waste when we could be living a lavish life.

Claim His promises and live a whole, healthy, and hopeful life.

You belong to the King of kings and Lord of lords. Stop living a pauper's life! Live as a child of the King.

November 6

Father, may Your name be kept holy.

—Luke 11:2, NLT

In heaven God's will is done, and the master teaches the child to ask that the will may be done on earth just as in heaven in the spirit of adoring submission and ready obedience.

Because the will of God is the glory of heaven, the doing of it is the blessedness of heaven. As the will is done, the kingdom of heaven comes into the heart (Andrew Murray).

> The Father reigns supreme above.
> The glory of His name
> Is Grace and Wisdom, Truth and Love.
> His will must be the same.
> And Thou has asked all joys in one,
> In whispering forth, "Thy will be done." (Frances R.
>   Havergal)

November 7

> I relied only on the power of the Holy Spirit.
>
> —1 Corinthians 2:4, NLT

I write the devotionals in a purple spiral notebook. My corner in the covered sunroom has books and materials strewn over the tables on either side of my chair.

Early mornings are my most productive. Later morning and early afternoon I transfer the writings to the computer and do research.

Some mornings, no matter how eager I am to write, I pick up the pen and find not one ounce of inspiration. I am in the way. I need to pray.

I don't come here depending on inspiration, Lord, for that would be depending upon myself. How foolish! I must yield, abandoning all thoughts and listening only to the sweet suggestions of Your Spirit in my soul. Mold me and fashion me into a vessel for Your honor. Less of me and more of You.

When we feel uninspired to do the work He has called us to do, we must yield to the Holy Spirit so that He may work in us by His own mighty power.

The Word of God brings us into spiritual life and sustains us. He is the author, and His Word has life-giving power.

November 8

> Rejoice in the Lord and be glad,
> all you who obey Him!
>
> —Psalm 32:11, NLT

The Lord waits for us to come to Him so He can show us His love and compassion. He is a faithful God, and we who know of His love are blessed.

We will hear His voice right behind us telling us the way we should go, whether to the right or to the left.

He directs our steps and delights in every detail of our life.

We stumble often, but we don't fall, for He holds us by the hand.

When we make His law our own, we will never slip from His path.

Today, we can put our hope in Him and travel steady along that path.

He has performed many wonders for us. His plans are too numerous to list.

You, O Jesus, have no equal. There is no one who compares to You!

If I tried to recite all Your wonderful deeds, I could never come to the end of them!

> Wheresoever God may lead you, there you will find Him, in the most harassing business, as in the most tranquil prayer.
>
> —Francois de la Mothe Fenelon

November 9

When I was a youngster, I was aware that most homes had a Bible. We did. I didn't see any of my family reading it. God's Word was read and preached on Sunday.

I liked looking in the front of the book at the pages my mother filled in: births, marriages, and deaths. Otherwise, the Bible lay on the table, unopened.

I was in my twenties when I became interested in reading the Bible. I joined a women's Bible study. A few of the women were spiritually mature, and I was impressed when they prayed Psalm 23 without reading it! Their example gave me a hunger for learning more of His Word.

That was only the beginning, and I have been abundantly fed by it. But just reading it or hearing it isn't enough.

In the Message version of the Bible, James 1:22–25 says, "Don't fool yourself into thinking that you are a listener when you are anything but, letting the Word go in one ear and out the other. *Act* on what you hear! Those who hear and don't act are like those who glance in the mirror, walk away, and two minutes later have no idea who they are, what they look like. But whoever catches a glimpse of the revealed counsel of God—the free life!—even out of the corner of his eye, and sticks with it, is no distracted scatter-brain but a man or woman of action. That person will find delight and affirmation in the action."

If you have even the slightest hunger to know God's Word, try a Bible study.

Your Word is a lamp for my feet, a light on my path.

—Psalm 119:105, NLT

November 10

> How sweet are Your words to my taste!
> *Yes, sweeter* than honey to my mouth!
>
> —Psalm 119:103, NASB

Lord God, You ask that I take joy in doing Your will, for it is in this that You delight. Yes, my joy brings You pleasure.

Your Word is written on my heart and is sweeter than honey to me. Your instructions give me understanding and are my treasure. I am grateful that Your Word gives light to even the simple like me, to help me understand what brings You delight.

Guide my steps by Your Word. Look upon me with love, and teach me Your decrees.

Let praise flow from my lips, for You have taught me what You want me to do. Let my tongue sing about Your Word, for all Your commands are right.

I will sing of Your unfailing love forever!

Let my lips utter praise,

For You teach me Your statutes.

Let my tongue sing of Your word,

For all Your commandments are righteousness (Ps. 119:171–172, NASB)

Your unfailing love will last forever.

We serve a mighty God who takes delight in us!

November 11

Child, you must listen to me when I say love your enemies!

Do good to those who hate you.

Bless those who curse you.

Pray for those who hurt you. If someone slaps you on one cheek, offer the other cheek also. If someone demands your coat, offer your shirt also. Give to anyone who asks, and when things are taken away from you, don't try to get them back.

Do to others as you would like them to do to you.

If you love only those who love you, why should you get credit for that? Even sinners love those who love them! And if you do good only to those who do good to you, why should you get credit? Even sinners do that much!

And if you lend money only to those who can repay you, why should you get credit? Even sinners will lend to other sinners for a full return.

Your reward waits for you, and you will be living the way I desire for you to honor Me.

Then your reward from heaven will be very great, and you will truly be acting as children of the Most High (Luke 6:27–35, NLT).

> Live by every word that comes
> from the mouth of the Lord.
>
> —Deuteronomy 8:3, NLT

November 12

> The Heavens proclaim Your glory O God.
>
> —Psalm 19:1, NLT

We watch the newscasts with wordless wonder as NASA's New Horizons spacecraft, which has traveled 3 billion miles, sends first-ever pictures of Pluto. Scientists say it appears to be no more than 100 million years old. In a solar system some 4.5 billion years old, they say that makes Pluto—which had been reduced to "dwarf planet" status in 2006—practically infantile.

David makes every effort in this psalm to tell of the craftsmanship of God. He uses images such as a tent for the sun, a radiant bridegroom, and an eager athlete. Those were the word pictures available to him.

The heavens are telling of the glory of God, and their expanse is declaring the work of His hands. Day to day pours forth speech, and night to night reveals knowledge.

There is no speech nor are there words; their voice is not heard. Their line has gone out through all the earth, and their utterances to the end of the world.

In them He has placed a tent for the sun, which is as a bridegroom coming out of his chamber; it rejoices as a strong man to run his course. Its rising is from one end of the heavens, and its circuit to the other end of them; there is nothing hidden from its heat (Ps. 19:2–6, NLT).

Space exploration, melded with the Word of God, give us a glimpse, no more than a minute grain of sand, at the expanse of God's mighty power as the heavens proclaim His glory!

To God be the glory forever and ever! Amen.

November 13

> The Lord detests lying lips, but He
> delights in those who tell the truth.
>
> —Proverbs 12:22, NLT

We all lie. To say, "I don't lie" *is* a lie.

In the broadest sense, lying ranges from the harmless to the harmful. Some white lies are common: lying about one's age or the size of the fish that got away. We reason that as long as no one gets hurt or the result is good, little white lies are fine.

When I was a youngster, it was a practice to cross our fingers behind our back when telling a white lie. I never did know why, but I've read that it may have its roots in the belief that the power of the Christian cross might save one from being sent to hell for telling a lie.

Then there was this: "Cross my heart and hope to die." I didn't understand that one either, but I used it! While saying it, we made a gesture over our breast, crossing our heart. It most likely originated as a religious oath based on the sign of the cross.

We learned at a young age that some lies are okay, but the Bible is clear that lying is a sin. The first sin in this world was by Satan. Jesus says that "When he lies, it is consistent with his character; for he is a liar and the father of lies" (John 8:44, NLT).

When we get caught in a lie, there may be a demand for another to cover the original lie. We scramble to remember who we told what to and when.

> Oh, what a tangled web we weave when first we practice to deceive.
>
> —Walter Scott

November 14

> My health may fail, and my spirit may grow weak, but God remains the strength of my heart; He is mine forever.
>
> —Psalm 73:26, NLT

When my twenty-five-year marriage ended in divorce, my life crumbled around me. I left my hometown and closed the doors on the home I had lived in for over twenty years where I raised my children.

I was now in unchartered territory. With trepidation, I faced being alone. I experienced debilitating bouts of anxiety, driven by fear of what the future held.

At times my grieving spirit seemed mired in spiritual darkness. It was one of those agonizing days when the reality of my losses seemed all consuming. I was despairing. I felt as though I was standing alone knee-high in a field of manure. I couldn't move. There was no one in sight, no houses, trees, animals—nothing. The blistering sun scorched the earth around me. The smell invaded my senses. I saw no way out of this quagmire. My eyes were cast down at the mess I was in. I felt helpless and hopeless.

Then only one sentence was available to me. I picked up a pen and wrote, "He subtracts all 'til none is left save Him." At that exact moment, as I read the words that my heart had given me, He became my *all*.

From this field of misery I looked up. I saw a brilliant red rose in full bloom. I could smell its fragrance instead of the stench in which I was standing. My eyes fixed on its beauty instead of the desolate landscape surrounding me. I raised my hand to reach for the rose. I was still in that field, but I no longer felt alone.

When circumstances catapult us from familiar surroundings, when dreams fall apart and things beyond our control have thrust us from our comfort zone, He is there.

He can restore our broken heart in a way we cannot imagine. We are safe in His arms when we make Him our all.

November 15

I had just finished a call with the graphic designer at Tate Publishing regarding the selection of the book cover for *Views from the Water's Edge*. It was the last detail to address before the book went to print. We agreed on the choice.

It was an incredible day; sunshine blanketed the shimmering blue water. I headed for a walk down the beach, grateful that there were only a handful of people with the same idea.

I walked about a mile and sat on the rocks. A few surfers dotted the water. The surf rolled on to the sand; pelicans soared over the waves. My senses were keenly aware of all that surrounded me. The cool breeze touched my face. I closed my eyes. I felt His pleasure. My heart and being were singing His praises for the result of the book's progress and the overwhelming reality that it had come this far. I was filled with gratitude, absorbing the precious moments with Him.

I looked over and saw something red lying there. I thought it was the strap from a surf board. I ignored it, but when I got up to leave, I walked over for a closer look. It was a long-stemmed red rose! Drops of ocean water glistened on its petals; wet sand clung to the inside and outside of the deep red beauty. It looked fresh!

Larry and I had seen some roses on the beach on our Saturday morning walk. They may have been there for a couple of days as they weren't looking very good. But this is Wednesday! One lone rose survived the high tide, the sun, and the Monday downpour? How could that be?

I picked it up—oh, my! The words sprung from within me. "He subtracts all 'til none is left save Him." Tearfully, I headed back down the beach, holding my rose and repeating those words. It had been twenty-nine years since I had written them.

> When you come to the end of all the light you know, and it's time to step into the darkness of the unknown, faith is knowing that one of two things shall happen: Either you will be given something solid to stand on or you will be taught to fly.
>
> —Edward Teller

November 16

> Not that we are adequate in ourselves to consider
> anything as coming from ourselves, but our
> adequacy is from God.
>
> —2 Corinthians 3:5, NASB

My teenage years were happy ones, but I spent a lot of time dwelling on my weight. In reflection, I may not have looked fat to my friends and family, but I felt fat. I heard once too often, "You're not fat; you're pleasingly plump."

We're occupied with weight. And we can become obsessed with shedding it.

Statistics tell us that the annual revenue of the US weight-loss industry, including diet books, diet drugs and weight-loss surgeries, is $20 billion. There are 108 million people on diets in the US Eighty-five percent of those consuming weight-loss products and services are female.

Some have been blessed with good genes and other factors that contribute to their physique. I'm not one of them. And so I watch my weight, what I eat, and how much.

One help for self-control came from the *Weigh Down Diet* by Gwen Shamblins. I took this prayer to memory and said if often throughout my day.

My diets were replaced with discipline. Focusing on God and not on food.

Lord, You made my body and set within me the amounts of fuel that are required to live. I pray that You would help me today to be sensitive to those amounts and not go beyond what is needed.

Lord, help me to let go of my focus on food so I will not lust for more than that.

Fill my thoughts instead with Your love and compassion so I do not feel yearning or greed, but contentment.

> So whether you eat or drink, or whatever
> you do, do it all for the glory of God.
>
> —1 Corinthians 10:31, NLT

November 17

Several friends are struggling with the realities of age. The calendar no longer has social engagements but is filled with doctor appointments. Their children are exploring the possibility of assisted living.

They are of strong faith, their lives devoted to serving God. They know that He loves them and will care for them, but fear of the unknown future can be debilitating.

Hebrews 13:5–8 assures us that "'I will never fail you. I will never abandon you.' So we can say with confidence, 'The Lord is my Helper; therefore I will have no fear.'"

Does God scold us when we are afraid? I don't think so. When a child is frightened, does the parent scold him for having no confidence in his father's protection? No. He draws him close, assuring him that it all will be okay and that he will take care of him.

And so our compassionate Father does for us. "There is no fear in love; but perfect love casts out fear" (1 John 4:18, NASB).

November 18

> My soul, wait in silence for God only,
>   for my hope is from Him.
>
> —Psalm 62:5, NASB

There is immense power in silence. It eludes most of us. And if you are raising a family, you may not remember what that is.

You might relate to this one. *Zits* is a comic strip about a high school teenager. One day he walked into the living room where his dad is sitting.

Zits: What are you doing?
Dad: What do you mean what I am doing?
Zits: I don't see an iPod, I don't hear any music, and the TV isn't even on!
Dad: I know. I'm just sitting her enjoying the silence.

Next we see Zits staring at his Dad, who now has his eyes
  closed.
Zits: No, seriously. What *are* you doing?

Some people seem to have an addiction to noise. The
coffee pot and TV go on simultaneously in the morning.
When the engine starts, so does the car radio.

And do you notice that no matter where we shop—
from the grocery store, to the mall, doctor, or dentist
offices—music (and not the "one size fits all" kind) intru-
sively invades the air. We're conditioned enough to not
even notice it anymore. But it's there.

Try turning off some of the noise in your life. Make time
for silence. We need to be listening to the Spirit that He
might control our lives, not the world.

Do you realize that *silent* and *listen* have the same letters?

November 19

> He has granted to us His precious
> and magnificent promises.
>
> —2 Peter 1:4, NASB

I was bored with the cereal I'd eaten for years and decided
to try a new one. So there I stood in the cereal aisle, reading
labels on at least ten boxes of cereal, each one promising

to be healthy, lower cholesterol, be good for my heart, and include more fiber (one bowl of this equals ten bowls of that). I gave the sugarcoated ones a glance. The one with chunks of chocolate was a huge temptation, certainly better than bran flakes. How long must I have looked at the multitude of choices?

We have so many choices that it leads to confusion. Manufacturers dress up their products, advertising them as though our lives will be empty without them. Oftentimes we buy the pretty package only to find it tasteless or useless.

I think of the times I've succumbed to the lure of what the world offers only to find my choice empty of the promise. I chose what looked good, not what was good for me.

Spiritual maturity brings us to the book of promises. God's Word is full of rich and soul-satisfying promises. Those of us with faith are promised that His divine power has granted us everything pertaining to life and godliness. This is not an empty promise!

I rely on Your promises, Father, not the empty promises of the world.

November 20

> Encourage those who are timid. Take tender care
> of those who are weak. Be patient with everyone.
>
> —1 Thessalonians 5:14, NIV

Lord, forgive me if this day I have done or said anything to increase the pain of others.

Pardon any unkind word, deliberate or unintentionally. I want to honor You in all my actions, showing sympathy and compassion, kindness, and generosity.

May I live each day aware of the opportunity to lesson someone's sorrow, taking time to listen.

Deliver me from any act or word that grieves You.

I know Your will for me is to be holy. Make me holy in every way, and may my whole spirit, soul, and body be kept blameless until You, Lord Jesus Christ, come again.

Do not make life hard to any.

—R. W. Emerson

November 21

Heavenly Father, when I am weary, draw me gently into Your loving arms. I look to You for refreshment and peace.

You promise You will never leave me nor forsake me.

As I surrender all to You, my strength will be renewed, and whatever You call me to do, You will provide the power and courage to move forward.

By a conscious act of my will, I turn to You, letting Your Spirit enter and control! I put my hope in You, resting secure and safe in Your loving arms

I will bless You, for You guide me; even at night my heart instructs me.

I know You are always with me. I will not be shaken, for You are right beside me.

No wonder my heart is glad, and I rejoice.

My body rests in safety.

You will show me the way of life, granting me the joy of Your presence and the pleasures of living with You forever (Ps. 16:11, NLT).

November 22

> Sing and make music from your heart to the
> Lord, always giving thanks to God the Father for
> everything, in the name of our Lord Jesus Christ.
>
> —Ephesians 5:19–20, NIV

With simplicity, my heart abides continually in communion with You.

I reflect on You with feelings of love and adoration.

I offer You all that I am.

When weaknesses or my unfaithfulness slip in and this conscious awareness of You dims, I humbly begin again.

You reach for me when I falter, and You lift me when I fall.

I meditate more on the things of eternity than the struggles here on earth. They are constantly in my thoughts. I cannot stop thinking about Your mighty works. This draws me ever closer to You.

I am making music to You in my heart.

As the deer pants for the water brooks,

so my soul pants for You, O God (Ps. 42:1, NASB).

November 23

Jesus, You healed many in Your earthly ministry. The leper, whose highly contagious disease made him an outcast and forced him to live outside the city, desperately and courageously kneeled before You, begging to be healed. "If You are willing, You can heal me and make me clean."

Moved with compassion, You touched him, restoring his deteriorating body. You came to restore life.

My life is scarred by sin, and I need healing. My sin has cast me away from You, robbing me of a life with You. But in Your compassion and love for me, You died that I might be healed and restored to life.

Like the leper, I come and kneel before You. If You are willing, You can heal me and make me clean. Renew me, strengthen me, guide me, and direct my thoughts, words, and actions.

Touch my soul and heal me. Purify my soul, renew my spirit, and give me a heart of compassion and love for all.

Heal me, gracious Lord, body and soul. But, most importantly, wash me, and I will be whiter than snow. Purify me from my sins, and I will be clean. That is true healing (Ps. 51:7).

November 24

> I will be filled with joy because of You. I will sing
> praises to Your name, O Most High.
>
> —Psalm 9:2, NLT

If we have a murmuring spirit, we can't have cheerfulness. It will generally show in our expressions and our voice. Some little agitation or restlessness of tone will betray it.

Cheerfulness can't be forced. It springs up freely from our heart, which it can only do when it is truly at rest in God. When we are rejoicing in Him, it is impossible not to be cheerful. For it is then that our heart and mind are so completely free that we can't help but rejoice in the Spirit.

Let us seek the grace of a cheerful heart, an even temper, sweetness, gentleness, and brightness of mind, as walking in His light, and by His grace.

—John Henry Newman

November 25

But He turned and said to Peter,
"Get behind Me, Satan!"

—Matthew 16:23, NASB

Child, no temptation has overtaken you except what is common to mankind. And I am faithful; I will not let you be tempted beyond what you can bear.

But when you are tempted, I will also provide a way out so that you can endure it.

Because I Myself suffered when I was tempted, I am able to help you when you are being tempted.

Blessed is the one who perseveres under trial because, having stood the test, you will receive the crown of life that I have promised to those who love Me.

When tempted, never say, "God is tempting me." For I cannot be tempted by evil, nor do I tempt anyone (James 1:12–13, NASB).

Submit yourself to Me. Resist the devil. Say, "Get behind me, Satan," and he will flee from you.

Hold to this promise!

> The soul which gives itself wholly and without reserve to God, is filled with His own peace; and the closer we draw to our God so much the stronger and more steadfast and tranquil shall we become.
>
> —Jean Nicolas Grou

November 26

> Well then, if you teach others, why
> don't you teach yourself? You tell others
> not to steal, but do you steal?
>
> —Roman 2:21, NLT

Larry and three-year-old Ashley went to the park down the street. He spotted a baseball lying in the grass. It was like new, and he picked it up.

"We can't take that, Grandpa."

"But somebody left it."

"It's not ours," she said.

"Well somebody else will find it and take it."

"It's not ours."

Smiling, he dropped it, scooped her up, and gave her one of those "grandpa" hugs.

My thoughts wander back to the five-acre farm we lived on when I was a youngster. Our neighbor's apple tree branches hung over the fence into our field. It was tempting to pick from his tree. *He won't miss one or two.* I want to say that I never did sneak one, but I can't say that.

If the room is filled with people from all walks of life and we are asked to examine our definition of stealing, there would probably be a variety of opinions. Justification of stealing has many sides, and at the end of the session, there probably won't be a unanimous decision of the meaning *to steal*.

Once a religious leader asked Jesus this question: "Good Teacher, what should I do to inherit eternal life?"

"To answer your question, you know the commandments: You must not commit adultery. You must not murder. You must not steal. You must not testify falsely. Honor your father and mother" (Luke 18:20, NLT).

According to God's commandments, stealing is right up there with adultery, murder, lying, and not honoring our father and mother.

Can we imagine our changed world with the childlike sense of right and wrong that Ashley had? "It's not ours."

November 27

> May the Lord's will be done.
>
> —2 Samuel 10:12, NLT

"Your will be done."

For instance, when we wish and do all that is possible to be well and yet remain sick, then we say "Your will be done."

When we undertake a task, committing everything we have to see it to completion and don't succeed, say, "Your will be done."

When we do a kind deed for someone and they repay with meanness, we say, "Your will be done."

Or when we long to sleep and can't, we say, "Your will be done."

The bottom line is not becoming irritated when anything is not done according to our will but learning to submit in everything to the will of God.

> The best will is our Father's will,
> And we may rest there calm and still
> Oh! Make it hour by hour thine own,
> And wish for naught that alone which pleases God.
>   (Paul Gerhardt)

November 28

> If you keep My commandments, you will abide
> in My love; just as I have kept My Father's
> commandments and abide in His love.
>
> —John 15:10, NASB

To lay up treasure in heaven is to do acts that promote or belong to the kingdom of God.

And what our Lord assures us of is that any act of our hands, any thought of our heart, any words of our lips that promotes the divine kingdom by the ordering, whether of our own life or of the world outside—all such activity, though may seem for the moment to be lost, is really stored up in the divine treasure house.

And when the heavenly city, the New Jerusalem, shall at last appear, that honest effort of ours, which seemed so ineffectual, shall be found to be a brick built into that eternal and celestial fabric.[20]

> We cannot remove the conditions under which our
> work is to be done, but we can transform them. They
> are the elements out of which we must build the
> temples wherein we serve.
>
> —Brooke Foss Westcott

November 29

> Is anyone among you suffering? Let him pray.
> Is anyone cheerful? Let him sing psalms.
>
> —James 5:13, NKJV

O Lord, You reign forever, executing judgment from Your throne. You will judge the world with justice and rule the nations with fairness.

You are a shelter for the oppressed, a refuge in times of trouble.

Those of us who know Your name, trust in You, O Lord. Do not abandon those who search for You.

I will sing praises to You and tell the world of Your unforgettable deeds!

I rejoice in Your unfailing love. You have not abandoned me when I sink into the mire with the major and minor challenges that I face. But when I turn to You, focusing on You, I can rise above it all.

I praise You because You bend down and listen to me.

You lift me, giving me guidance in every detail of my life.

I will listen to You, accepting all You have to say, all You would have me do.

You are my Lord and my God! I praise you!

Your Word is a lamp for my feet, a light on my path.

—Psalm 119:105, NLT

November 30

Her love for him was all consuming. Everything was dictated by her hopeless need for him. But he didn't love her. He dabbled briefly in the relationship and then pulled away. She shattered, and nothing mattered.

Unrequited love. The raw emotion of desperate love finds solace in nothing else.

My life was ripped apart by such love. I had lost myself in it, and when the relationship was severed, I had lost my self-worth. The sting of unrequited love is not forgotten.

Is it any wonder that I have come to lose myself to the One who loves me most? I have never known such love. He fulfills all my needs and loves me unconditionally.

He is faithful, trustworthy, perfect, patient, gracious, and kind to me. He is pure, wise, loving, and compassionate. He knows me intimately and fulfills my every need. My love for Him is all consuming.

He has given me joy, hope, faith, peace, and strength. He fills me with His power, discernment, and tranquility. His grace is sufficient for all I need.

I have found unconditional love, and I have found self-worth in Him.

And I am convinced that nothing can ever separate me from His love. Neither death nor life, neither angels nor demons, neither my fears for today nor my worries about tomorrow—not even the powers of hell can separate me from His love (Rom. 8:38, NLT).

December 1

I love You, Lord; you are my strength. You are my Rock, in whom I find protection. You are my Shield, the power that saves me, and my place of safety

You light a lamp for me. You light up my darkness.

Your way is perfect. All of Your promises prove true.

You arm me with strength, and You make my way perfect.

You make me as sure-footed as a deer, enabling me to stand on mountain heights. You have made a wide path for my feet to keep them from slipping.

The Lord lives! Praise to my Rock!

May the God of my salvation be exalted!

You have endowed me with eternal blessings, and given me joy in Your presence.

I trust in You, O Lord. Your unfailing love will keep me from stumbling.

I give my life to You, my God. You are holy and righteous, worthy to be praised (Ps. 18:1–3, 28, 30–33, 46, NLT).

December 2

> Even before there is a word on my tongue,
> Behold, O Lord, You know it all.
>
> —Psalm 139:4, NASB

Dear Father, a difficult truth for me to comprehend is that
  You, the God of the universe
are a personal God to me.
You care for me, concerned about every feeling and emo-
  tion, every move that I make.
You know my heart; read my mind.
You know what I'm going to say and do before I do.
No, I don't understand, and I cannot fathom such a God.
But by faith I know it to be so.
I know because of the evidence of Your presence in my life.
You and I have an intimate relationship.
I treasure that, my Lord and my God.

> How sweet Your words taste to me;
> they are sweeter than honey.
>
> —Psalm 119:103, NLT

December 3

I praise You for mornings like this. I woke feeling the joy of Your presence.

I shout joyfully to You, O God.

I sing the glory of Your name.

How awesome are Your works.

You are my shepherd, and I have all I need.

This day, You will let me rest in green meadows bursting with beauty and intoxicating fragrance.

You will lead me beside peaceful streams, and I will sit in tranquility.

You will renew my strength and guide me on the right path that I need to take.

Oh, yes, I embrace the joys of this day, for You are with me, and my cup overflows with Your grace. Alleluia!

December 4

> Faithful is He who calls you, and
> He also will bring it to pass.
>
> —1 Thessalonians 5:24, NASB

Is it hypocritical to pray when we don't feel like it?

Waiting until we are in the mood to pray can hinder our communion with almighty God. It deprives us of all that is necessary to abide in Him. What shall we do when moods like this come?

If we waited until we are in the mood to clean the house, grocery shop, do laundry—the list goes on—would any of it get done? We end up with a dirty house, little food, and a hamper filled with soiled clothes.

When we don't feel like praying, it is the time we need most to pray. The only way we will overcome little interest in prayer is to put more of ourselves into it. Praying when we don't feel like praying is not hypocrisy; it is faithfulness to the duty to which God has called us.

If we aren't in the mood to pray, we should tell God. At least we are talking to Him. That's prayer!

> When you cannot pray as you would, pray as you can.
>
> —Charles H. Spurgeon

December 5

> Pharaoh and all his officials and all the Egyptians got up during the night, and there was loud wailing in Egypt, for there was not a house without someone dead.
>
> —Exodus 12:30, NIV

The exodus is worth our taking a second look.

"Get out!" he ordered. "Leave my people—and take the rest of the Israelites with you! Go and worship the LORD as you have requested. Take your flocks and herds, as you said, and be gone. Go, but bless me as you leave."

The Egyptians urged the people to hurry and leave the country. "For otherwise," they said, "we will all die!"

So the people took their dough before the yeast was added and carried it on their shoulders in kneading troughs wrapped in clothing. The Israelites did as Moses instructed and asked the Egyptians for articles of silver and gold and for clothing. The Lord had made the Egyptians favorably disposed toward the people, and they gave them what they asked for.

The Israelites journeyed from Rameses to Sukkoth. There were about six hundred thousand men on foot, besides women and children. Many other people went up with them and also large droves of livestock, both flocks and herds. With the dough the Israelites had brought from Egypt, they baked loaves of unleavened bread. The dough was without yeast because they had been driven out of Egypt and did not have time to prepare food for themselves.

Now the length of time the Israelite people lived in Egypt was 430 years. At the end of the 430 years—to the very day—all the Lord's divisions left Egypt. Because the Lord kept vigil that night to bring them out of Egypt, on this night all the Israelites are to keep vigil to honor the Lord for generations to come.

We serve a mighty God!

December 6

I fall to my knees and pray to You, the Father, the creator of everything in heaven and on earth.

I pray that from Your glorious, unlimited resources You will empower me with inner strength through Your Spirit. Then You will make Your home in my heart as I trust in You.

My roots will grow down into Your love and keep me strong. May I have the power to understand, as all Your people should, how wide, how long, how high, and how deep Your love is.

May I experience Your love, though it is too great to fully understand. Then I will be made complete with all the fullness of life and power that comes from You, my Lord and my God! (Eph. 3:14–19, NLT)

December 7

Solomon continually spoke to God. Lord, I join my voice with him in prayer.

Give me wisdom and knowledge

Teach me to realize the brevity of life so that I may grow in wisdom (Ps. 90:12, NLT).

You are the strength of my life.

Each day You pour Your unfailing love upon me, and I sing songs of praise to You who gives me life.

You forgive all my sins and crown me with love and tender mercies. You fill my life with good things.

You are my God, and I will exalt You.

Oh, how great is Your wisdom.

I fervently live for You, knowing my life is like the morning fog; it is here for a little while and then it is gone (James 4:14, NLT).

> The grass withers and the flowers fade,
> but the Word of our God stands forever.
>
> —Isaiah 40:8, NLT

December 8

Heavenly Father, I know that I am not here by chance but by Your choosing.

Your hand has formed me and made me the person I am.

I am unique, one of a kind.

I lack nothing, for Your grace provides all I need.

You have given me life, to be here at this time and place to fulfill Your purpose in me.

In spite of all my failures, You continue to lift me up so that my life will complete all You would have me to do while I am on this earth.

I look forward to the heavenly reward You have promised me. Someday I will be with You.

> Then may Thy glorious, perfect will
> be evermore fulfilled in me,
> And make my life an answering chord
> of glad, responsive harmony. (Jean Sophia Pigott)

December 9

> I can do all things through Him who strengthens me.
>
> —Philippians 4:13, NASB

O Lord, I am disheartened by the troubles around me. I fear that Satan is wining this battle. I cry to You for help. I am conscious of my weakness and the strength of the enemy.

You are in me and I in You. So with a deliberate exercise of my will, I surrender in faith to You, drawing upon Your strength and not on my own resources.

By focusing on You and releasing these unstable emotions, I am victorious over Satan! I praise You, my Lord and my God.

> Some of us believe that God is all mighty, and may do all, and that He is all wisdom, and can do all, but that He is all love, and will do all, there we fail.

> —Mother Juliana

December 10

We visited the Rijksmuseum in the Netherlands. I sat on the bench in front of Rembrandt's *The Night Watch*. My eyes tried to capture the essence of such a work, but they couldn't. His self-portraits and biblical scenes on display left me with wordless marvel. No wonder museums are so quiet!

While I know nothing about painting, I find pleasure in looking at the work. The painter is gifted and creates a masterpiece from artistic passion and inner inspiration. A fellow artist can view a painting and value the intricacy far more than I. I do appreciate its beauty but would be hard-pressed to discuss the complexity of such a painting with an artist who is equally gifted.

And so it is with God. Those who have a deep personal relationship with Him study His awesome beauty, taking in all of His wonder, His glory, and His majesty! They have a profound appreciation of who He is. They sit before Him with wordless marvel.

There are those who appreciate God and know Him on some levels. Their appreciation of Him coincides with the depth of their relationship with Him.

Father, I lift my eyes to You, enthroned in heaven. You are the artist! You, who created everything in heaven and on earth and all that is in the sea. You, who stretched out the sky like a canopy and laid the foundations of the earth!

You created me in Your image and likeness, Your masterpiece! You have created me anew in Christ Jesus so I can do the good things You planned for me long ago (Eph. 2:10).

I gaze upon Your work with wordless marvel.

> Every artist dips his brush in his own soul, and paints his own nature into his pictures.
>
> —Henry Ward Beecher

December 11

> And He has made my feet like hinds' *feet*,
> and makes me walk on my high places.
>
> —Habakkuk 3:19, NASB

Habakkuk lived in Judah during a time of oppression and persecution. Wicked, evil kings had been on the throne; the country was in a state of lawlessness and immorality. The prophet couldn't understand why God continued to allow such evil to exist.

After agonizing over the devastating results such evil would do to his country, he recognized his limitations in contrast to God's unlimited power over all things.

> Though the fig tree should not blossom and there be no fruit on the vines,
> though the yield of the olive should fail and the fields produce no food,
> though the flock should be cut off from the fold and there be no cattle in the stalls, yet I will exult in the Lord,
> I will rejoice in the God of my salvation. The Lord God is my strength, and He has made my feet like hinds' feet, and makes me walk on my high places."
> (Hab. 3:17–19, NASB)

We live in a world of evil and injustice. Yet, like Habukkuk, we can rejoice that we are not controlled by events surrounding us but by faith in a just God. God is alive; He is in control. We can't see all that He is doing, but we can be assured that if we place our trust in Him and not in man, we will be sure-footed in these difficult times. We will walk on high places.

Oh, Lord God, help me to take my eyes off the events around me and look only to You.

December 12

> When you meet them and see their behavior, you
> will understand that these things are not being
> done to Israel without cause. I, the Sovereign Lord,
> have spoken!
>
> —Ezekiel 14:23, NLT

The outward features of our life may not be all that we should choose them to be. There may be things we wish for that never come to us; there may be much we wish away that we cannot part from.

The persons with whom we live, the circumstances by which we are surrounded, the duties we have to perform, and the burdens we have to bear may not only be other than what we should have selected for ourselves but may even seem inconsistent with that formation and discipline of character which we honestly wish to promote.

Knowing us better than we know ourselves, fully understanding how greatly we are affected by the outward events and conditions of life, He has ordered them with a view to our entire and final—not only our immediate—happiness. And whenever we can be safely trusted with pastures that are green and waters that are still in the way of earthly blessing, the good shepherd leads us there.[21]

December 13

Child, you are My sheep, listen to My voice. I know you, and am delighted that you follow Me. I give you eternal life, and you will never perish. No one can snatch you away from Me, for My Father has given you to Me, and He is more powerful than anyone else. No one can snatch you from My Father's hand (John 10:27–29, NLT).

You, O Lord, are my shepherd! I cannot comprehend this. You seem so far away yet so close. I yearn to know more about You.

I come before You in humble prayer knowing that You, the omnipotent God, love me. Who am I that You should be mindful of me? I am frayed in every way. Yet You invite me through Your Word to come unto You, to seek after You, love You, and to follow You.

O God, that is what I want, yet I don't always do that. I live in a world that draws me away from all that You ask of me. You have richly blessed me with those whom I love and who love me. Yet they can take my attention away from You. Am I to sit hour upon hour in Your presence, to come with no earthly attachments and loves? Is that what You ask of me?

You abide in me and I in You.

I will rest in the knowledge that no one can snatch me away from You. And every thought directed toward You brings me closer to You.

Yes! I am Your sheep, and I am in my Father's hand.

December 14

Father, shift my thinking.
Shake all prejudice from me.
Adjust my established priorities.
Bend Your ear to my supplications.
Saturate my whole being with Your Spirit.
Quench my thirst by Your presence.
Satisfy this longing for You, O God.
Wipe away discouragement and sadness.
Pour Your unfailing love over me.
Lift me from the petty annoyances that distract me.
Take from me all that You will and give me what I need.

December 15

Who couldn't feel sorry for Moses? When God called him to deliver His people from slavery and lead them to the Promised Land, Moses went kicking and screaming.

"I can't do that, Lord God! I am not capable!" God told him He would help him. For forty years Moses put up with a grumbling and rebellious people. After all of that, God denied him entrance into the Promised Land.

Even knowing that he would not be with them, Moses reviews the covenant God had made with His people. He reminds them of God's faithful love for them, freeing them from slavery. He instructed them that the key to life is to love and obey God and commit themselves firmly to Him (Deut. 30:19–20, NKJV).

When Moses had finished giving these instructions to all the people of Israel, he said, "I am now 120 years old, and I am no longer able to lead you. The LORD has told me, 'You will not cross the Jordan River.' But the LORD your God Himself will cross over ahead of you. He will destroy the nations living there, and you will take possession of their land. Joshua will lead you across the river, just as the LORD promised" (Deut. 31:1–3, NKJV).

No matter what Moses was dealt, he praised his God to the end. "For I proclaim the name of the LORD: Ascribe greatness to our God. *He is* the Rock, His work is perfect;

For all His ways are justice, a God of truth and without injustice; righteous and upright is He" (Deut. 32:3–4, NKJV; emphasis mine).

Can we say that? Will we praise Him even when He says no?

December 16

> The sun will be darkened, the moon will give
> no light, the stars will fall from the sky, and the
> powers in the heavens will be shaken.
>
> —Matthew 24:29, NLT

And then at last, the sign that the Son of Man is coming will appear in the heavens, and there will be deep mourning among all the peoples of the earth. And they will see the Son of Man coming on the clouds of heaven with power and great glory. And He will send out his angels with the mighty blast of a trumpet, and they will gather His chosen ones from all over the world—from the farthest ends of the earth and heaven.

Now learn a lesson from the fig tree. When its branches bud and its leaves begin to sprout, you know that summer is near. In the same way, when you see all these things, you can know His return is very near, right at the door. No one knows the day or hour when these things will happen, not even the angels in heaven or the Son Himself. Only the Father knows.

When the Son of Man returns, it will be like it was in Noah's day. In those days before the flood, the people were enjoying banquets and parties and weddings right up to the time Noah entered his boat. People didn't realize what was going to happen until the flood came and swept them all away. That is the way it will be when the Son of Man comes.

Two men will be working together in the field; one will be taken, the other left. Two women will be grinding flour at the mill; one will be taken, the other left.

So you too must keep watch! For you don't know what day your Lord is coming. Understand this: If a homeowner knew exactly when a burglar was coming, he would keep watch and not permit his house to be broken into. You also must be ready all the time, for the Son of Man will come when least expected (Matt. 24:30–44, NLT).

The very essence of Your words is truth.

—Psalm 119:160, NLT

December 17

> About midnight Paul and Silas were praying and
> singing hymns to God, and the prisoners were
> listening to them.
>
> —Acts 16:29, NLT

Charles Spurgeon writes:

Any man can sing in the day. When the cup is full,
man draws inspiration from it.

When wealth rolls in abundance around him,
any man can praise the God who gives a plenteous
harvest.

The difficulty is for music to swell forth when no
wind is stirring.

It is easy to sing when we can read the notes by
daylight, but he is skillful who sings when there is not
a ray of light to read by—who sings from the heart.

Lay me upon the bed of languishing, and how
shall I then chant God's high praises unless He
Himself gives me the song?

No, it is not in man's power to sing when all is
adverse, unless an altar-coal shall touch his lip.

Then, since our maker gives "songs in the night,"
let us wait upon Him for the music.

December 18

I like bridges. A popular tourist attraction in my hometown, Cañon City, Colorado, is the Royal Gorge Bridge, which spans the Arkansas River at a height of 1,053 feet. It was the world's highest suspension bridge from 1929 until 2001. I have walked across the 1,292 planks of the wooden walkway. It's thrilling and scary!

I have seen Jesus depicted as a bridge—the bridge that connects us to God. It is a visual to help me understand my need of Him as a mediator between God and me.

Man had rejected God in the Garden of Eden, turned from Him and followed his own way. He disobeyed God, and God used Christ to restore His relationship with humanity. The Bible says that Christ reconciled us to God. The fact that we needed reconciliation means that our relationship with God was broken. Our sin alienated us from Him. "And all of this is a gift from God, who brought us back to Himself through Christ, for God was in Christ, reconciling the world to Himself, no longer counting people's sins against them" (2 Cor. 5:18–19, NLT)

I know that God sent Jesus as a savior to bridge the gap between man and Himself. We are sinners. It is our choice to cross the bridge that spans our connection with God. There is a deep chasm below. We must keep our eyes focused on the other side. He is waiting for us there.

December 19

> I beseech you therefore, brethren, by the
> mercies of God, that you present your
> bodies a living sacrifice, holy, acceptable to
> God, *which is* your reasonable service.
>
> —Romans 12:1, NKJV

I have read, "There was no rudder to Noah's ark." He didn't need one. He had obeyed God and closed the doors of the ark. If God ordered it, He would steer it.

We think of the ridicule Noah had endured for years as he built the ark. There were some who thought him to be crazy. But Noah remained faithful.

Dr. S. D. Gordon writes, "God could give to Abraham, because he had made such a wide opening into his life. God can give only into an open hand. This hand was open wide. This door swung clear back. God had a free swing and He used it. He could, and He did. He always does.

"Let this be our rule: Give all He asks, then take all He gives. And the cup will be spilling joyously over the brim."

Yes, Lord! Take what You want and give me what You want me to have.

December 20

Child, my desire for you is that you live your life with purpose. If you heed My words, your life can make a difference to many.

For I know the plans that I have for you: plans for welfare and not for calamity, to give you a future and a hope. Then you will call upon Me and come and pray to Me, and I will listen to you. You will seek Me and find Me when you search for Me with all your heart (Jer. 29:11–13, NASB).

I urge you to offer your body as a living sacrifice, holy and pleasing to Me. Do not conform to this world but be transformed by the renewing of your mind. Then you will be able prove what My will is for you. It is always good, pleasing, and perfect.

Use the gifts with which I have blessed you. Everyone has different gifts, according to the grace given. If your gift is prophesying, then prophesy in accordance with your faith; if it is serving, then serve; if it is teaching, then teach; if it is to encourage, then give encouragement; if it is giving, then give generously; if it is to lead, do it diligently; if it is to show mercy, do it cheerfully (Rom. 12:6–10, NASB).

Whatever I ask of you, wherever I may send you, do it willingly. Seek My kingdom, and I will give you all you need to accomplish My will for you, that your life will be filled with lasting purpose.

Commit yourself wholeheartedly
to these words of Mine.

—Deuteronomy 11:18, NLT

December 21

Ponderings:

- "You can have hope without faith, but you cannot have faith without hope!" (Randy Furco)
- "Faith is to believe what we do not see, and the reward of faith is to see what we believe" (St. Augustine).
- "Discontentment makes rich men poor while contentment makes poor men rich" (Benjamin Franklin).
- "To handle yourself, use your head; to handle others, use your heart" (Eleanor Roosevelt).
- "All things proclaim the existence of God" (Napoleon).
- "Pain, suffering and death are already enough trials in our lives without adding the consequences of sin" (Richard Strauss).
- "Prayer is not conquering God's reluctance, but taking hold of God's willingness" (Phillips Brooks).
- "The smallest act of kindness is worth more than the greatest intention" (Kahlil Gibran).

December 22

I know my worth comes from You alone, O God. I humbly call on Your power and seek Your guidance, surrendering my independent efforts.

I don't deserve Your favor, O God, but You reach out in love giving me worth and dignity in Your sight despite my human shortcomings.

Yours, O Lord, is the greatness, the power, the glory, the victory, and the majesty. Everything in the heavens and on earth is Yours, and this is Your kingdom.

Wealth and honor come from You alone.

Power and might are in Your hands. You are the ruler of all things, and at Your discretion, people are made great and given strength (1 Chron. 29:11–12, NASB).

Who am I that I could give anything to You? Everything I have has come from You, and I give you only what You first gave me! I am here for only a moment, a visitor and stranger. My days on earth are like a passing shadow, gone so soon without a trace.

December 23

Child, there is no condemnation for those who belong to Me. And because you belong to Me, the power of the life-giving Spirit has freed you from the power of sin that leads to death (Rom. 8:1, NASB).

I sent My own Son in a body like the bodies you have as sinners. And in that body I declared an end to sin's control over you by giving My Son as a sacrifice for your sins.

When you follow the desires of your sinful nature, you die to Me. But if, through the power of my Spirit, you put to death the deeds of your sinful nature, you will live.

You can't do that on your own, but by My power you will regard the appeal of sin as lifeless—dead!

I have adopted you as My own; You call Me Abba, Father. You are heir to My glory together with Jesus.

Think of it.

My Spirit joins with Your spirit to affirm that you are Mine.

> Commit yourself wholeheartedly
> to these words of Mine.
>
> —Deuteronomy 11:18, NLT

December 24

Every Christmas we assemble our small Dickens Village at the base of the revolving Christmas tree. It's a tranquil place: lighted merchants' shops, people on benches wave to passersby, and plenty of snow-covered pine trees and lighted street lamps. And there's the church. A manger scene sits in front.

It is my habit during this season to sit here for my early morning quiet time. This morning I imagine the village bursting with life. All of my immediate family together, living in peace and harmony. Each one brings their unique talent and gifts that make a community of selflessness and service. There are no arguments, no jealousy, nor competition. Each of us is filled with faith in Jesus Christ, bound in our love for Him. I read John 17:20–23, when Jesus is praying to His Father, and wonder, "Do I have to imagine this?"

"I am praying not only for these disciples but also for all who will ever believe in Me through their message. I pray that they will all be one—just as You and I are one—as You are in Me, Father, and I am in You. And may they be in Us so that the world will believe You sent Me. I have given them the glory You gave Me so they may be one as We are one. I am in them, and You are in Me.

May they experience such perfect unity that the world will know that You sent Me and that You love them as much as You love Me."

I join in Jesus's prayer, and make it our family prayer, knowing of our faith in Him and secured by His love for each one of us.

Can you imagine your family living in the serene Dickens Village?

December 25

> And there were shepherds living out in the fields
> nearby, keeping watch over their flocks at night.
> An angel of the Lord appeared to them, and the
> glory of the Lord shone around them, and they
> were terrified.
>
> —Luke 2:8–9, NIV

They were the first to hear the news of the birth of the King. The glory of God shone down on shepherds! Lowly shepherds, whose lives reflect sacrifice, were the first to kneel before Jesus, the long-awaited Messiah.

Jesus told the crowds, "I am the Good Shepherd and I lay down My life for the sheep. I know My own sheep, and they know Me, just as My Father knows Me and I know the Father. So I sacrifice My life for the sheep" (John 10:11, 15, NIV).

The crowds understood about the shepherd's life. Sheep are defenseless and totally dependent upon the shepherd. They are subject to sudden heavy rainfalls that could sweep them away, robbers who may steal them, and wolves that may attack. Shepherds spent long lonely hours each day, and were frequently subjected to danger, sometimes even giving their lives to protect their flock.

Jesus came to earth in human form in order for us to know what God is like. And as the Good Shepherd, He willingly laid down His life to pay for our sins. The wonder of His birth, first proclaimed to shepherds, reveals His very nature.

He is the Shepherd, we are the sheep—defenseless and totally dependent upon Him.

Let us humbly bow before Him as the shepherds did that night. We know Him to be the King of kings, Lord of lords, and our Shepherd!

Glory to God in highest heaven, and peace on earth to those with whom God is pleased!

December 26

Larry and I both came from humble beginnings. He entered the workforce at a young age, holding numerous jobs.

Work! The word is used often in the Bible.

I like Paul's take on it. "Those unwilling to work will not get to eat" (2 Thess. 3:10, NLT).

There's a difference between leisure and laziness. Relaxation provides a necessary and much-needed balance to our lives, but when it is time to work, Christians should jump right in. We should make the most of our talents and time doing all we can to provide for ourselves and our dependents.

Larry and I are blessed to have retired from the workforce, having more time to work for the Lord.

"But the godly will flourish like palm trees and grow strong like the cedars of Lebanon. Even in old age they will still produce fruit, they will remain vital and green" (Ps. 92:12, NLT).

> O, blest retirement! Friend to life's decline—
> How blest is he who crowns, in shades like these,
> A youth of labor with an age of ease! (Oliver Goldsmith)

December 27

> Those who say they live in God should
> live their lives as Jesus did.
>
> —1 John 2:6, NLT

I pray I will be conscious of Your presence at all times. It brings calm in the most common duties and kindness in my encounter with others. Even the minutest detail will be offered to You as sweet aroma.

Unwanted interruptions will not be intrusions, but I will consider them as coming from You so that I might meet them with patience.

Then I will know I am living as You desire, by Your power working in me.

I will become what You would have me to be because You live in me and I in You.

"Now he who keeps His commandments abides in Him, and He in him. And by this we know that He abides in us, by the Spirit whom He has given us" (1 John 3:24, NKJV).

> I have no cares, O Blessed Will!
> For all my cares are Thine;
> I live in triumph, Lord, for Thou
> Has made Thy triumphs mine. (Frederick W. Faber)

December 28

> You are my light and salvation, whom shall I fear?
> You are the defense of my life; whom shall I dread?
>
> —Psalm 27:1, NASB

The one thing I ask of You, Lord—the thing I seek most—is to live in Your house all the days of my life, delighting in Your perfections and meditating upon You.

For You will conceal me there when troubles come.

You will hide me in Your sanctuary.

You will place me out of reach on a high rock.

Then I will hold my head high above my enemies who surround me.

I will offer sacrifices with shouts of joy, singing and praising You with music (Ps. 27:4–6, NASB).

Hear me as I pray, O Lord.

Be merciful and answer me!

December 29

> The Lord is like a father to His children, tender
> and compassionate to those who fear Him.
>
> —Psalm 103:13, NLT

Don't measure God's mind by your own. It would be a poor love that depended not on itself but on the feelings of the person loved. A crying baby turns away from its mother's breasts, but she does not put it away 'til it stops crying. She holds it closer.

For my part, in the worst mood I am ever in, when I don't feel I love God at all, I just look up to His love. I say to Him, "Look at me. See what state I am in. Help me!"

Ah! You would wonder how that makes peace. And the love comes of itself, sometimes so strong it nearly breaks my heart.[22]

He does not love us because we art so lovely,
but because He always loves what He pities.

—Elizabeth Prentiss

December 30

Look! I stand at the door and knock. If you hear
My voice and open the door, I will come in, and
we will share a meal together as friends. Those
who are victorious will sit with Me on My throne,
just as I was victorious and sat with My Father on
His throne.

—Revelation 3:20–21, NLT

Child, be still; listen.

Do you hear My voice asking that I might come in and abide in you?

Open the door to your heart.

Invite Me in.

Do you understand the unspeakable joy you will know as you sit with Me on My throne?

Don't shut Me out.

I love you and want to have fellowship with you.

I want you to feel My presence in your life.

And if God knocks continually at the heart of man, desiring to enter in and sup there, and to communicate to him His gifts, who can believe that when the heart opens and invites Him to enter He will become deaf to the invitation, and refuse to come in?

—Lorenzo Scupoli

December 31

Just as you cannot understand the path of the wind or the mystery of a tiny baby growing in its mother's womb, so you cannot understand the activity of God, who does all things.

—Ecclesiastes 11:5, NLT

Discouraged and inadequate. Those are just two of the major obstacles I have encountered while writing this book. Waves of discouragement have tested my faith.

I question how that can happen when I spend hours in the scriptures.

I have come to believe that any undertaking that has been commissioned by the Lord can be obstructed. We are vulnerable to attack by Satan as was Jesus.

But we cling to the promise that He will not leave us. He will not change when our moods swing out of control.

He will hold us firmly so that we do not crumble under the tasks we have been given.

"My thoughts are nothing like your thoughts," says the Lord. "And My ways are far beyond anything you could imagine. For just as the heavens are higher than the earth, so My ways are higher than your ways and My thoughts higher than your thoughts" (Isa. 55:8–9, NLT).

Thank you for the assurance that You, O Lord, are faithful to complete the good work in us.

The task ahead is no greater than the power behind you.

—Unknown

NOTES

1. George Hodges, Mary Wilder Tileston, compiler. *Joy and Strength* (Minneapolis: World Wide Publications, 1901), p. 1.
2. Alexander McKenzie, Mary Wilder Tileston, compiler. *Joy and Strength* (Minneapolis: World Wide Publications, 1901), p. 251.
3. Forward Day by Day, (Forward Movement, Cincinnati).
4. Francis Paget, Mary Wilder Tileston, compiler. *Joy and Strength* (Minneapolis: World Wide Publications, 1901) p. 249.
5. Brother Lawrence, *The Practice of the Presence of God* (Grand Rapids: Revell, Baker Book House, 1958).
6. Hannah Whitall Smith, Mary Wilder Tileston, compiler. *Joy and Strength* (Minneapolis: World Wide Publications 1901), 242.
7. H. L. Sidney Lear, Mary Wilder Tileston, compiler. *Joy and Strength* (Minneapolis: World Wide Publications 1901), 178.

8. Claire Cloninger, *Containers: Filled with God*, Daily Thoughts, Internet.

9. Edward B. Pusey, Mary Wilder Tileston, compiler. *Joy and Strength* (Minneapolis: World Wide Publications 1901), 49.

10. St Catharine of Siena, Mary Wilder Tileston, compiler. *Joy and Strength* (Minneapolis: World Wide Publications 1901), 36.

11. John Henry Newman Mary Wilder Tileston, compiler. *Joy and Strength* (Minneapolis: World Wide Publications 1901), 84.

12. Anthony de Mello, S. J., *The Song of the Bird* (Image Books, 1984), 164.

13. Mrs. Charles Cowman, compiler, *Springs in the Valley* (Grand Rapids: Daybreak Books 1939, 1968), 333.

14. Andrew Murray, Mary Wilder Tileston, compiler. *Joy and Strength* (Minneapolis: World Wide Publications 1901), 15.

15. Jack Wheaton, Commentary, Jack Wheaton's Online Bible Study.

16. Edward B. Pusey, Mary Wilder Tileston, compiler. *Joy and Strength* (Minneapolis, MN: World Wide Publications 1901), p. 230.

17. Paul R. Van Gorder, *Power From on High*, Radio Bible Class.

18. Millie Stamm *Prayer, Talking with God* (Stonecroft Book & Media Ministries, 1988), 9.
19. William R. Huntington, Mary Wilder Tileston, compiler. *Joy and Strength* (Minneapolis: World Wide Publications 1901), 199.
20. Charles Gore, Mary Wilder Tileston, compiler. *Joy and Strength* (Minneapolis: World Wide Publications 1901), 240.
21. Anthony W. Thorold, Mary Wilder Tileston, compiler. *Joy and Strength* (Minneapolis: World Wide Publications 1901), 17.
22. George Macdonald, Mary Wilder Tileston, compiler. *Joy and Strength* (Minneapolis: World Wide Publications 1901), 217.